D1135447

AROUND THE WORLD IN

80

NOVELS

Published in 2019 by CICO Books
An imprint of Ryland Peters & Small Ltd
20–21 Jockey's Fields   341 E 116th St
London WC1R 4BW   New York, NY 10029
www.rylandpeters.com

10 9 8 7 6 5 4 3 2 1

Text © CICO Books 2019
Design © CICO Books 2019
For picture credits, see page 160.

ISBN: 978 1 78249 663 2

Printed in China

Editor: Alison Wormleighton
Designer: Geoff Borin

Art director: Sally Powell
Production controller: Mai-Ling Collyer
Publishing manager: Penny Craig
Publisher: Cindy Richards

WIDE SARGASSO SEA

THE AGE OF INNOCENCE

CAPTAIN CORELLI'S MANDOLIN

AROUND THE WORLD IN

80

NOVELS

A global journey inspired by writers
from every continent

HENRY RUSSELL

TALES OF THE CITY

THE GOOD EARTH

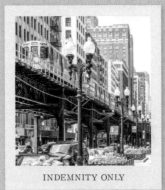

INDEMNITY ONLY

CICO BOOKS
LONDON NEW YORK

CONTENTS

INTRODUCTION

*"A first-rate page-turner"... "Powerfully resonant"...
"Breathtaking"... "Impossible to recommend too highly"... "An
immense achievement"... "Absolutely brilliant"... "Sensuous and
thought-provoking"... "Sensitive, daring, deeply moving"... "Vivid,
moving, and absorbing"... "Stunning"...*

These are just some of the puffs on the covers of the novels featured in this book. They were extracted by their publishers from newspaper and magazine reviews in the hope of increasing sales. But what do they tell potential buyers about the actual content? Nothing. So how can people decide what to read?

If you are contemplating a trip, but not yet sure where you want to go, novels may help you make up your mind – but which ones? Or if you already know where you want to go, which works of prose fiction will increase your understanding and enjoyment of the intended destination? *Around the World in 80 Novels* suggests some possible answers to these questions.

The choices have been carefully considered, but author and publisher are under no illusion that the list will meet universal approval. There's no accounting for taste, and arguments about what's good in the arts—perhaps including a certain amount of controversy—are no bad things.

At the planning stage we considered doing one book per country, but soon found that unsatisfactory. Therefore some countries have several entries, while many have only a single representative. The United States has nine while Canada and Russia, though much larger, have only two each. Perhaps

that seems a bit arbitrary, but we reasoned that the sparsely populated belt that goes most of the way around the Earth between the 49th and 75th parallels has less variety—and indeed is the setting for fewer novels—than the contiguous 48.

Although deciding what countries to include was a problem, agreeing on which books to omit was an even bigger headache. Many great novels with a strong sense of place—*Don Quixote; The Sorrows of Young Werther; War and Peace; Adventures of Huckleberry Finn*—didn't make the cut, either because they're too well known already or because any edition with larger than microscopic print will take up too much room in the carry-on baggage. That said, we admit there's some inconsistency here—several of the chosen works are big—but decisions had to be made. We can only hope that you approve.

Some of the featured works describe their settings in minute detail. Patrick Modiano's Paris is laid out with satnav-like precision. Daphne du Maurier and Zora Neale Hurston wrote guidebooks to the locations that inspired them (Cornwall and Florida, respectively), and that expertise informs their fiction.

Other choices are short on topography but capture the spirit of their nation. In placing

An Artist of the Floating World in a generic setting that might be anywhere in Japan, Kazuo Ishiguro deftly evokes the whole of the country. The French village in *Chocolat* is a product of Joanne Harris's imagination, but plenty of her readers think that they've been to it—indeed, that they've stayed there; her novel is in some ways *plus français que la France*. Isabel Allende is coy about the setting for *The House of the Spirits*—she claims it could be any country in South America—but it's hard to imagine that anyone who'd read about or visited Chile would not recognize it in her masterpiece.

Some of the books are set in times gone by, but that doesn't reduce their relevance to the modern visitor. The past is in the present whenever we think about it, and in many places it's impossible to prevent it from springing to mind: all over Flanders and northern France, World War 1 is memorialized more than a century after the conflict ended, and the sense of history that pervades the region is captured in Sebastian Faulks's *Birdsong*. For any visitor to Vietnam seeking historical context, Bao Ninh's *The Sorrow of War* should be considered essential reading.

Several books in the following pages make the places they describe seem idyllic: for example, Croatia in Ann Bridge's *Illyrian Spring*, and Botswana in Alexander McCall Smith's *The No. 1 Ladies' Detective Agency*. More often, however, there is danger abroad, especially in the thrillers, yet fictional evil does nothing to deter bookish visitors—if anything, it attracts them to the place. In making Ystad the setting for his murder mysteries, Henning Mankell turned a small Swedish port into a noted tourist center. Similarly, the critical acclaim accorded Harper Lee's *To Kill a Mockingbird* transformed its setting, a rural Southern US backwater, into "the Literary Capital of Alabama."

CITY OF GOD

It is hoped that every book featured here will crank up the reader's wanderlust.

Inspired, of course, by *Around the World in 80 Days*, we take in the countries visited by Phileas Fogg—France, Italy, Egypt, India, China, Japan, the United States, and Ireland—as well as England, Fogg's start and end point, and dozens of other nations, some of which didn't exist when Jules Verne's novel was published in 1873.

Henry Russell
London, 2019

The author thanks Meredith Jones Russell for her help with Russian matters.

WUTHERING HEIGHTS

CAL

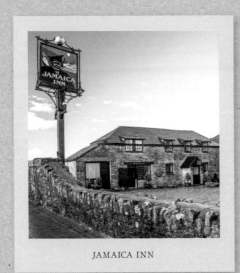

JAMAICA INN

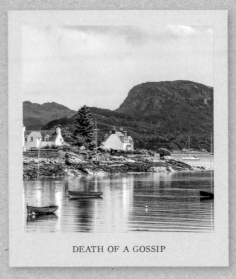

DEATH OF A GOSSIP

CHAPTER 1

UNITED KINGDOM AND IRELAND

SCOTLAND

KIDNAPPED (1886)

ROBERT LOUIS STEVENSON

Kidnapped first appeared in serial form in *Young Folks*, a children's weekly magazine. The work was well received by reviewers at the time, but some later critics deprecated it as no more than an adolescent tale of derring-do. In their view, Robert Louis Stevenson (1850–94) was the weakest of the three Titans of Scottish literature, scarcely worthy of mention in the same breath as Robert Burns and Walter Scott.

Republished as a novel, *Kidnapped* has never been out of print and is now firmly established in the pantheon. Readers who demand seriousness have come to see the work as a study of the nature of honor. Those who seek a realistic context are satisfied that the fiction is woven around a historical event: the 1752 Appin Murder of Colin Campbell, nicknamed the Red Fox, an agent sent by the English king, George II, to extract revenue from the Scots after their defeat at the Battle of Culloden (1746).

But those who count readability among the loftiest literary virtues have always rated Stevenson highly. Although *Kidnapped* contains words and phrases unfamiliar outside Scotland (but not too many, as the work's original editor demanded), no idiom or vocabulary is so arcane as to distract from the rapidly unfolding drama.

The action begins when the hero, 17-year-old David Balfour, sets out into the world after the death of his parents. He walks from his family home in the Scottish Lowlands to Edinburgh, there to meet his uncle for the first time—his expectations of this encounter do not include the attempt on his life that follows. It fails but the wicked old man then tricks his nephew onto the *Covenant*, a ship bound for North America, where, it is intended, David will be sold into slavery.

As the vessel sails around the north of Scotland, bound for the Atlantic, it accidentally hits a smaller vessel and rescues the sole survivor, Alan Breck, a boastful and dandyish but brave and noble Scotsman in French uniform.

On learning that the *Covenant*'s captain and crew plan to rob their new passenger, David and Alan form an alliance. After a mortal onboard struggle the ship is driven aground and the pair escape onto Erraid, a small island off the western edge of Mull.

Stevenson's prose is unflagging in its pace and unfailingly evocative of the terrain: "Now we ran among the birches; now stooping behind low humps upon the mountain-side; now crawling on all fours among the heather…" It's a warts-and-all depiction, though—he even mentions midges, the bane of many Scottish summers.

David Balfour's subsequent route back to Edinburgh has since become known as the Stevenson Way—230 miles (370km) across the still-wild heart of central Scotland. It's not signposted, partly because the original text is vague about the exact itinerary, but with a good map the broad outline is easy to follow: eastward from Erraid, through Morvern, across Loch Linnhe to Ballachulish, through Glencoe into the

Rannoch Moor wilderness, and thence to the slopes of Ben Alder; then south to Loch Rannoch, through the mountains above Bridge of Orchy to Crianlarich, over the mountains to Loch Voil and Balquhidder, then to Callander, Dunblane, Stirling, and Limekilns, and finally across the Firth of Forth to the Scottish capital. David and Alan parted company on Edinburgh's Corstorphine Hill, and since 2004 there has been a statue of them nearby.

ABOVE *Here at Bridge of Orchy, the Stevenson Way (which runs roughly west–east from the small island of Erraid, just off the Isle of Mull, to Edinburgh) intersects the West Highland Way (running north–south between Milngavie and Fort William).*

SCOTLAND

DEATH OF A GOSSIP (1985)

M. C. BEATON

This is the first in what became a series of more than 30 lighthearted detective stories by M. C. Beaton, one of the pen names of Scottish author Marion Chesney (b. 1936). Chesney has also written romance novels under the names Sarah Chester, Helen Crampton, Ann Fairfax, Jennie Tremaine, and Charlotte Ward.

Death of a Gossip is set in the fictional Highland village of Lochdubh. Eight people enroll on a course at the local School of Casting to learn how to fish for the trout and salmon that thrive in the local waters. Seven of these students have guilty secrets while the eighth, Lady Jane Withers, is a nasty newspaper gossip columnist hell-bent on exposing the others' dirty linen to public scrutiny. It is no surprise to any—and a relief to some—of them when this muck-raking writer turns up dead; she has been murdered.

On the trail of the killer goes Hamish Macbeth, the local bobby whose most readily apparent characteristics are indolence and an overwhelming desire to avoid promotion. Although his investigative methods are idiosyncratic and sometimes eccentric, he turns out to be something of a super-sleuth who cracks the case with the help of his longtime girlfriend, Priscilla Halburton-Smythe. (Whether these two will ever marry becomes a running theme in subsequent books.) The only person who doesn't think highly of Hamish's abilities is his direct superior and would-be nemesis, Chief Inspector Blair from police headquarters in the nearby town of Strathbane

(also fictional). The two officers come into regular conflict, and the constable outwits the top brass every time.

Based on some of the Beaton novels, *Hamish Macbeth* was a version for television (three series, a total of 20 episodes) that ran from 1995 to 1997. It was written by Daniel Boyle and starred Robert Carlyle. Much of the location filming was in Plockton, a stunningly beautiful village on the shores of Loch Carron with a station on the scenic "Kyle Line" (the Inverness–Kyle of Lochalsh railway). Now a popular site of pilgrimage for fans of the series, Plockton markets itself as "the Jewel of the Highlands."

AGATHA RAISIN

The prolific Marion Chesney, again writing as "M. C. Beaton," is also the author of more than 20 novels of which the heroine is a retired public relations officer turned amateur sleuth who solves crime in England's Cotswolds area. *Agatha Raisin*, an eight-part television series based on some of these books, was broadcast in 2015 and starred Ashley Jensen in the title role. As this book went to press, a second series had reportedly been commissioned and was starting production.

ABOVE *Now most famous as the location for the television series* Hamish Macbeth, *Plockton had appeared on screen before, notably in the 1973 horror film* The Wicker Man.

KNOTS AND CROSSES (1987)

IAN RANKIN

The Edinburgh of this novel is a dark city thrown into panic by a serial killer who targets young girls. One of the detectives assigned to the case is John Rebus, who is ex-SAS (Special Air Service, the British army's commando force), divorced and tormented by his past. He has a teenage daughter and a brother who is a drug dealer. Among the other significant characters are Gill Templer—John's girlfriend and a fellow police officer—and Jim Stevens, a boozy newspaper reporter.

The general gloom of the setting is intensified by the protagonist himself: saturnine, sarcastic, fatalistic, and psychologically damaged, John Rebus comes under suspicion of committing the crimes he's investigating. He is an ambivalent, potentially sinister figure. Ian Rankin (b. 1960) later stated that part of his inspiration for *Knots and Crosses* was Robert Louis Stevenson's *Strange Case of Dr Jekyll and Mr Hyde* (1886), a work he admired but felt should have been set in the Scottish rather than the English capital because it was based on a "real-life Edinburgh character… who was gentleman by day, criminal by night." (He was referring to Deacon William Brodie, a diurnal cabinetmaker and city councilor who was hanged in 1788 for his nocturnal activities as a house burglar.)

At first Rankin had no intention of writing detective fiction—indeed, he claims he didn't know that *Knots and Crosses* was even of that genre—but this novel, though largely unnoticed on first publication, gradually grew in popularity and spawned more than 20 sequels and a television series. In *Exit Music* (2007), Rebus reached 60, retirement age in the police force, and many people assumed that was the last of the series, but there have since been five further volumes to date, most recently *In a House of Lies* (2018).

LEFT *Unlike many Edinburgh pubs, The Oxford Bar has not been modernized: a deliberate decision by the owners to keep it as described in the Rebus novels.*

In his introduction to the 2005 edition of *Knots and Crosses*, Rankin remarked that the Edinburgh he described in the book "no longer exists." But that's only partially true. Some of the locations in the novels are invented, others are fictional conflations of more than one place, and a few have since closed—yet a number of places are the same today as they appear in the books. The unintended consequence has been a burgeoning Rebus tour industry.

Near the beginning of *Knots and Crosses*, Rebus and his colleague Jack Morton go out to drown their sorrows. Rankin writes, "They drank in some of Edinburgh's seedier bars, bars the tourist never sees." That's no longer the case. Among the highlights of the many trips now on offer around the Scottish capital are Rebus's tenement building at 24 Arden Street, The Oxford Bar in Young Street, and the Police Station at 14 St Leonard's Street.

NAMING OF PARTS

Not everyone approves of literary labels, but those who think they're useful have lumped all modern Scottish crime writers who may plausibly be described as "gritty" into a genre called Tartan Noir. The earliest novel to which this term has been applied is *Laidlaw* (1977) by William McIlvanney, which is set in Glasgow. *Knots and Crosses* is widely held to be the second in line. The crime fiction of Val McDermid may also be categorized as Tartan Noir.

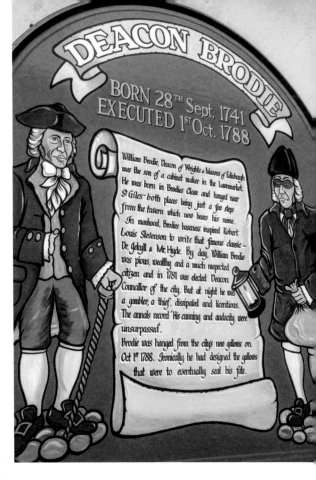

ABOVE *This mural outside the tavern on Edinburgh's Lawnmarket commemorates Deacon William Brodie, the real-life hero–villain who Rankin once suggested could have been the inspiration for Stevenson's* Strange Case of Dr Jekyll and Mr Hyde, *which in turn had partly inspired* Knots and Crosses.

WUTHERING HEIGHTS (1847)

EMILY BRONTË

This extraordinary novel that combines Gothic horror with Victorian social realism is set in the heart of Yorkshire and has become a universally recognized emblem of the wildest parts of that great English county.

A complex story of the power of love in both its destructive and regenerative forms, it all stems from the time when old Mr Earnshaw brought home to his manor house, Wuthering Heights, a young waif he'd found wandering the streets of Liverpool. This dark, brooding presence, whom his adoptive father names Heathcliff, has a big impact on Earnshaw's own children: his son Hindley sees a rival for his parents' attention; his daughter Catherine falls madly in love with the newcomer, who is roughly the same age as she. The rest of the narrative charts the enduring consequences of the introduction of this cuckoo into the nest.

The setting is the landscape that Emily Brontë (1818–48) knew well: fictionalized versions of the countryside around Cowan Bridge, where she lived for a short time as a child; of the Shibden Valley where she worked as a schoolteacher; and— most strikingly—of the terrain around Haworth, the town in which she spent the greater part of her life, which most commentators agree is near her imagined location of Wuthering Heights.

Prominent throughout this novel are the Yorkshire moors—wild lands that defy cultivation because they are either too dry or, as mainly here, too wet. All that grows there is heather. They have no fixed landmarks; it is easy to lose your way on them, and if you wander off the beaten track, there is always the danger of sinking into a bog and drowning.

Emily Brontë's most frequently quoted description of the moors occurs in the final paragraph of *Wuthering Heights* ("I lingered around them under that benign sky…" which is reproduced in almost every book of literary criticism and many quotation anthologies). However, similar passages occur throughout the book, as in the following quotation:

"…the whole hill-back was one billowy, white ocean; the swells and falls not indicating corresponding rises and depressions in the ground: many pits, at least, were filled to a level; and entire

BRONTË PARSONAGE MUSEUM

Haworth is a magnet for fans of Emily Brontë and her novelist sisters: Charlotte, author of *Jane Eyre* (1847), and Anne, author of *The Tenant of Wildfell Hall* (1848). The most important site in the town is the parsonage, where the family lived because their widowed father was the vicar of Haworth Church. The parsonage was where the sisters wrote their great works, and it is where their furniture, clothes, and possessions remain in place and on display to this day.

ABOVE *The remains of Top Withens, thought to be the inspiration for the Earnshaw home, look ominous even on the nicest days.*

ranges of mounds, the refuse of quarries' on one side of the road, at intervals of six or seven yards, a line of upright stones, continued through the whole length of the barren: these were erected, and daubed with lime on purpose to serve as guides in the dark; and also when a fall, like the present, confounded the deep swamps on either hand with the firmer path..."

Of course, the landscape has a figurative significance—it mirrors the emotions of the main characters, and its wildness reflects both Heathcliff's character and Catherine's passion for him—but what Emily Brontë describes is also what she saw, and what the visitor to Haworth and environs may still experience today.

HOUSE OF INSPIRATION

A not-too-difficult 1½ mile (2.5km) walk westward from the Parsonage leads to Top Withens, a farm that is widely supposed to have been the model for the Earnshaw family home.

HERITAGE TRANSPORT

Although Haworth is easily accessible by road, it can also be reached at a leisurely pace by steam train on the preserved Keighley and Worth Valley Railway. This line links with the national rail network at Keighley station on the Airedale Line between Leeds and Skipton.

ENGLAND
BLEAK HOUSE (1853)
CHARLES DICKENS

It may seem odd that a novel published in 1853 should continue to shape the expectations of first-time visitors to London. That it remains the case is attributable mainly to the descriptive power of Charles Dickens (1812–70). However, it is also partly because throughout the Cold War (c. 1945–89) Victorian works were some of the most recent English literature that people in the Communist bloc were permitted to read. Even a generation after the Iron Curtain was demolished, censorship still casts an influential shadow.

Bleak House is principally (but by no means exclusively) a satire of the law's delay: all the characters depicted are in some way involved in a dispute about a will that has spiraled into a case of such complexity and duration ("Fair wards of court have faded into mothers and grandmothers") that no one any longer knows what the case is really all about. (And in the not entirely unexpected dénouement, when the litigation is finally resolved, all the vast inheritance turns out to have been spent on professional fees.)

The part of the English capital in which the main action of the novel takes place—an area bounded on the south by the Strand, on the north by High Holborn, on the west by Kingsway, and on the east by Chancery Lane—is still today much as it was in the 19th century, although the district's most famous buildings, the Royal Courts of Justice, were not completed until 1882, 12 years after the author's death.

The work opens with a description of London rain that creates a sea of mud and "a general infection of ill temper" among the citizens as they jostle along the streets, banging their open umbrellas. There is fog everywhere. After Esther Summerson (one of two narrators; the other is an omniscient voice) first entered the capital, she noted that "the streets were so full of dense brown smoke that scarcely anything was to be seen." When she asked about it she was told, "This is a London particular."

And indeed it was: the depiction is grounded in reality. Ever since the 13th century, London had been notorious for its fogs, which hung heavy over the city and surrounding marshlands in the valley of the River Thames. After the Industrial Revolution, these clouds were thickened by smoke from factories to create smog that could reduce the horizon to the end of one's nose and that caused, particularly in winter, innumerable respiratory ailments. What became known as "pea soupers" enveloped London for at least a few days almost every year from Dickens's time until the mid-20th century. In 1952, a particularly bad occurrence caused the deaths of 10,000 people. Then government legislation, starting with the Clean Air Act of 1956, forced a reduction in open coal fires, though this was insufficient to prevent another smog in December 1962. Since then, London has become one of the world's cleaner major cities, but its reputation as a smog bowl has

persisted. This has been reinforced in enduring films, particularly some of those about Jack the Ripper, of which Alfred Hitchcock's *The Lodger* (1927) was an influential example.

What may sometimes be overlooked is that in *Bleak House* Dickens was conscripting the weather for figurative purposes: the mud is messy and the fog impenetrable, just like the lawsuit in the book, referred to as Jarndyce and Jarndyce. *Bleak House* evokes London but it is no Baedeker-like description—the city has always had sunny intervals.

ABOVE *On High Holborn in London, the Tudor building known as Staple Inn is the last surviving Inn of Chancery. Originally attached to London's four Inns of Court and used as offices for the Clerks of Chancery, the Inns of Chancery had by Dickens's time become, in effect, just glorified dining clubs for the legal subculture satirized in* Bleak House.

JAMAICA INN (1936)

DAPHNE DU MAURIER

At the southwestern extremity of mainland Britain, surrounded on all but one side by sea, Cornwall has long been a law unto itself—and sometimes lawless, too. Its criminal practices are what Daphne du Maurier (1907–89) highlights in this enduringly popular work.

The setting is Bodmin Moor, in the center of Cornwall. At the heart of this windswept, barren heathland of around 80 square miles (200 sq km) is the real-life hotel of the title, where du Maurier stayed in 1930. In the novel, which is set in the early 19th century, it is run by Joss Merlyn and his wife Patience. When the heroine, Mary Yellan, comes to live with this couple after the death of her mother, Patience's sister, she soon discovers that the place does not make its money in the way one might expect, from travelers on the main east–west highway beside which it stands. Instead, its income comes from clandestine nocturnal activities that Joss—a strong, angry, violent drunk—is insistent Mary should keep her nose out of.

But Mary is curious, and even if she weren't, it would be hard not to notice some of the goings-on. She soon concludes that the stock-in-trade of Jamaica Inn is smuggling, and up to a point she is right, but she later learns that what is going on is even worse than she has suspected.

That is one of the themes of the novel: that sometimes even our greatest fears fail to anticipate the full horror of reality. The fact that a do-gooding clergyman is to criminals as Jamaica Inn is to Bodmin Moor—right at the cold heart—is not anti-religious, but merely an observation that Mary, like many of us, is most deceived by that in which she puts the greatest faith.

Du Maurier's descriptive writing is so strong and prominent that the reader might wonder if the weather and the landscape actually determine the characters' mental state, rather than, as in most fiction, reflect it. One moorland feature is depicted as bursting out of the earth like a devil's hand. Such imagery has done nothing to put people off visiting Cornwall. The county remains a popular vacation destination long after many other British resorts have lost out to cheap European package tours—and the real-life Jamaica Inn is one of the area's principal attractions.

INN 'FLUENCE

In the book, honest, God-fearing travelers hurry past Jamaica Inn because they know or feel it's an evil place—the best advice to them is "Cross your heart and spur your horse." Nothing could be farther from the modern reality. The hotel thrives on its associations with the bestseller itself and the film and TV versions of it, especially the 1939 movie directed by Alfred Hitchcock. The real-life premises have a du Maurier room, which contains the author's writing desk and other du Maurier memorabilia; a museum housing smuggling artifacts; Haunted Rooms in which you can stay; ghost hunts; and monthly Murder Mystery evenings.

CORNISH SOUL

Daphne du Maurier had lifelong links with Cornwall. Her family vacationed there throughout her childhood, and in 1926, when she was 19, they bought Ferryside, a house in the village of Fowey. Following her marriage in 1932, she and her children spent vacations in Cornwall, and then in 1942 they settled permanently in Fowey. For the first year du Maurier rented Readymoney Cottage, but in 1943 she obtained a lease on Menabilly, just outside of Fowey. Since childhood, du Maurier had known and loved the mansion, which was one of the inspirations for Manderley in her 1938 novel *Rebecca*. After her lease on Menabilly expired, in the late 1960s, the widowed du Maurier lived for the rest of her life at Kilmarth, a house in the nearby village of Tywardreath, which became the setting for her 1969 novel *The House on the Strand*.

In *Vanishing Cornwall* (1967) du Maurier recounted some of the legends and pre-Christian lore of the local people. She lamented the dilution of the traditional Cornish ways by improved transport and increased contact with the world east of the River Tamar (the boundary with the only adjacent county, Devon). But the literary merit of this book inspired many people to use it as a guidebook, and thus encouraged the very tourism that the author deplored.

ABOVE *Jamaica Inn is a halfway house between the Cornish towns of Launceston, 12 miles (19km) to the northeast, and Bodmin, 10 miles (16km) to the southwest.*

ENGLAND
WHITE TEETH (2000)
ZADIE SMITH

If *Bleak House* is the London that first-time visitors expect, *White Teeth* is the London that they are more likely to encounter if they venture away from the tourist-focused center to the parts that lie outside the Underground Circle Line.

The setting is Willesden, a district on the northwestern outskirts of the capital where people of many religions and ethnicities coexist, largely peacefully, although it's not a tension-free zone. It might be described as a melting pot but Zadie Smith (b. 1975) is too original to use such a stale term. She has a vigorous voice and a sharp ear that help her to write dialogue which, even if not authentic, has a consistent ring of truth. It's often funny, too, especially when it reflects regional variants of English spoken by people of Asian and West Indian heritage.

BELOW *Willseden Green station opened in 1879, as a stop on the Metropolitan Railway. Today, only the Jubilee line usually stops here.*

At the heart of a story that encompasses much of the world in the last century, as well as a large chunk of British colonial history, are the conflicting and often irreconcilable desires of immigrants to assimilate into their adopted societies, to maintain their family traditions, and to reject their parents' values. Some of the characters here, like the Jehovah's Witnesses, cling fast to the old ways. Others weigh English customs in the balance—a Bengali at the local school's harvest festival wants to know, "Where in the Bible does it say, 'For thou must steal foodstuffs from thy parents' cupboards and bring them into school assembly, and thou shalt force thy mother to bake a loaf of bread in the shape of a fish'?" A son of pious Muslims reacts against his parents by studying law and becoming more English than the English—or, as his father puts it, "You show them the road and they take the bloody path to the Inns of Court." At the end of the book there is some suggestion that, as hard as these people may strive to shape their destinies, fate is never really under their control.

There are problems of integration. White middle-aged Archie gets taken off the invitation list for his work colleagues' outing after he marries a young black woman. His boss explains, "It's not that I'm a racialist," it's just that other members of staff "don't know what to make of that at all." When a trendy liberal white woman asks a Cockney Bengali where he's from "originally," he puts on a Peter Sellers-type mock accent: "Oh... You are meaning where from am I originally" and then gives it to her straight: "Whitechapel... Via the Royal London Hospital and the 207 bus."

TRIANGULATION

White Teeth is set in what is now a predominantly middle-class residential triangle. The point of the triangle is at the southeast, at Kilburn Underground station. The triangle's base, along the northwest edge of the area, is the North Circular Road (A406). The two sides of the triangle are the Metropolitan Underground line along the southern flank, and Shoot-Up Hill (A5) along the northeastern flank. In the center of the area is Gladstone Park, the highest point of which offers views of Wembley Stadium and the City of London.

HOW GREEN WAS MY VALLEY (1939)

RICHARD LLEWELLYN

This story of a mining family in South Wales during the reign of Queen Victoria is full of period and regional detail. The people use typically Welsh–English expressions and phrasing—such as "Are you in good voice with you?" or "Drink, is it?"—and some critics regard the Welsh countryside as one of the novel's leading characters.

The tone is wistful and nostalgic: the valley was green, but it is no longer. Nevertheless, one of the author's premises is that the past exists in the present whenever we call it to mind: "… there is no fence or hedge round Time that has gone. You can go back and have what you like if you remember it well enough."

The 1941 film version, directed by John Ford and starring Roddy McDowall, Maureen O'Hara, and Walter Pidgeon, enhanced the reputation of an already popular book and disseminated a stereotype of Welshness that in some quarters is taken for granted as accurate to this day.

In 1999, researchers looking for ways to celebrate the 60th anniversary of the original publication created a small storm by claiming that Richard Llewellyn (1906–83) was rather less Welsh than he would have had the world believe. The blurb on the back of the first Penguin edition (1951) of How Green Was My Valley states that the author was born in St David's, Pembrokeshire. But according to the then-BBC Wales producer Arwel Ellis Owen, Llewellyn was born in Hendon, north London, and his knowledge of mining came, not directly, as he claimed, but from a family named Griffiths who had left the valleys years previously to run a bookshop in London's Charing Cross Road.

Meic Stephens, poet, translator, and editor of The Oxford Companion to the Literature of Wales, described Llewellyn as a "semi-detached Welshman" who spun a myth about "a never-never land of pristine innocence ruined by the discovery of coal." While acknowledging that Llewellyn's myth spawned many of the stereotypes that followed in other works—singing miners, pit explosions— Stephens also observed that it was "a good yarn."

Llewellyn denied having a birth certificate, claiming that the non-registration of his birth had been his Welsh nationalist grandparents' protest against an English custom. When asked how, in that case, he knew his own age, he said that his date of birth had been entered into a family Bible that was lost when the family home was bombed during World War 2.

Some say that this made-up heritage renders Llewellyn's work valueless. But many people make unverifiable claims about their ancestry, and to criticize a novel for being a work of the imagination seems as perverse as dismissing Hamlet on the grounds that Shakespeare never visited Denmark.

The author's biography need have no bearing on our assessment of his work. Regardless of where Llewellyn was born, How Green Was My Valley inspires nostalgia in those who know or

have ancestral roots in Wales, and promotes it to those who have yet to discover its beauties for themselves.

ABOVE *Like many towns of South Wales, Ferndale (Welsh name: Glynrhedynog) in the Rhondda Valley was built in a valley formed by hills from which coal was extracted between the 1850s and the 1980s. Views such as this are part of an image of Wales that Llewellyn's novel helped to consolidate in the popular imagination.*

NORTHERN IRELAND

CAL (1983)

BERNARD MACLAVERTY

Ever since it was hived off from the Republic of Ireland in the 1920s, Northern Ireland has been a theater of political, religious, and ethnic conflict. Yet the resulting violence was sporadic until a civil rights movement to end discrimination against the Roman Catholic minority by the Protestant majority sparked the undeclared war known as the Troubles. It lasted from 1969— when the British army was sent in to restore and maintain order—until 1998, when it was officially deemed to have been ended by the Good Friday Agreement between the main belligerents and other interested parties.

Cal, a novel of around 60,000 words by Bernard MacLaverty (b. 1942), is set in Northern Ireland in the 1970s, the darkest period of the Troubles. The protagonist, Cal McCluskey, 20, has quit his job in an abattoir because the smell makes him vomit. Depressed and on welfare, he lives with his widowed father in a Protestant area in which they are the only remaining Roman Catholics. They get plenty of threats but the old man is too stubborn to move house.

Cal falls in love with Marcella, a librarian who is 10 years his senior—not that she notices at first, as he is too shy to approach her. He just hangs around her place of work, where the learned books on the shelves reinforce his already strong sense of inadequacy.

Cal is apolitical, but his old classmate Crilly, an ardent Republican and a violent bully, cajoles him into driving a getaway car in a shop robbery.

Cal says that's it, he'll do no more, but Crilly tells him that anyone who isn't for the cause is against it, and reminds him what happens to those who step out of line.

Cal reluctantly agrees to drive when Crilly goes out to kill a Protestant reserve officer of the Royal Ulster Constabulary. Although Crilly describes the target as "the greatest bastard unhung," what

RIGHT *One of the Peace Walls in Belfast that kept the warring factions apart during the Troubles and are now tourist attractions.*

he doesn't mention is that the intended victim is Marcella's husband.

Later, Cal and Marcella get to know each other properly and they start an affair. Cal wants to tell her everything but knows he never can. Crilly is arrested and, we infer, grasses on his accomplice. When the police knock at Cal's door, it comes to him as a blessed relief from his guilt, and he is "grateful that at last someone was going to beat him to within an inch of his life."

MacLaverty is unerringly nonpartisan: *Cal* demonstrates that there is right and (more particularly) wrong on both sides. That everyone and everything involved gets hurt is reflected in a livestock motif running throughout the book.

When Cal says he can't stand the slaughterhouse, his father—who also works there and who got him the job—tells Cal that if he had stuck it out he'd have got used to it, thus implying that one can become inured to anything. Significantly, the reader is not told at the start what species of animal is being killed, as if to suggest that death doesn't mind whether it takes animal or human, Protestant or Catholic, Republican or Loyalist, the innocent or the guilty. Later, a landmine intended for a human blows up a cow—an incident that is emblematic of futility and waste.

ULYSSES (1922)

JAMES JOYCE

This novel by James Joyce (1882–1941) is held by many to be one of the few works of art to succeed in capturing the vagaries of human thought processes—the habit of mind that digresses unbidden from the main agenda into loosely connected associated ideas, and that finds likenesses in unlike things.

The action takes place on a single day (June 16, 1904) and is a parallel to the *Odyssey*, the Greek epic poem of the 8th century BCE attributed to Homer. The three main characters in *Ulysses*—Stephen Dedalus, Leopold Bloom, and his wife, Molly—are 20th-century counterparts of, respectively, Telemachus, Odysseus (of which "Ulysses" is the Latin equivalent), and Penelope. But whereas Homer's creations are heroic, Joyce's are often preoccupied with petty concerns.

For example, the eighth of the 18 "episodes" in *Ulysses* is based on Odysseus' encounter with the Lestrygonians, a race of man-eating giants who terrorize a Mediterranean island. Joyce turns this incident into a description of Leopold Bloom's pangs of hunger as he walks through the center of Dublin. His growling stomach makes his mind wander off into ruminations about the political, cultural, and social significance of food and inspires the thought that "Peace and war depend on some fellow's digestion."

Part of Joyce's achievement lies in the way he manages stream-of-consciousness prose without losing sight of the world outside his characters' heads. Few works of literature are set more deeply in a particular place than Ulysses is set in Dublin. No. 7 Eccles Street, the Blooms' address, still exists. Although the current building on the site postdates *Ulysses*, the original door was salvaged by Joyceans and is now preserved at the James Joyce Centre in North Great George's Street.

Dublin is *Ulysses* as much as *Ulysses* is Dublin, and today guided tours of the Irish capital take in a host of locations where important and memorable events in the novel are set. The Lestrygonians episode takes place between Middle Abbey Street and the National Library. On O'Connell Bridge, Leopold Bloom buys Banbury cakes from a street trader and feeds them to the gulls. The Davy Byrnes pub on Duke Street is where Bloom has his lunch (a gorgonzola sandwich and a glass of Burgundy—a combination that is still, non-coincidentally, on the tavern menu today). At the

LEFT *The entrance to the James Joyce Centre, a short walk from Parnell Street in central Dublin.*

junction of Molesworth Street and Dawson Street, Bloom helps a blind man across the road—"He touched the thin elbow gently: then took the limp seeing hand to guide it forward."

There are many more such locations throughout the city, as well as several places of importance in Joyce's life, which have also become literary pilgrimage destinations. Among these is Belvedere College in Denmark Street, the exclusive Jesuit school where the author was a scholarship pupil.

For fans of Joyce, Dublin is a year-round cornucopia, but perhaps the best day to visit is June 16, which is now celebrated annually in Ireland and beyond as Bloomsday.

IRELAND

THE COMMITMENTS (1987)

RODDY DOYLE

The Commitments, the first novel written by Roddy Doyle (b. 1958), is set in the 1980s in Barrytown, a fictionalized version of the poor suburb of north Dublin where Doyle was a teacher. Some unemployed youths set out to form a band, and they advertise in a music paper for like-minded soul musicians. Phone applicants get asked one question—"Who're your influences?"— and thus the wheat gets sorted from the chaff. "—U2.—Simple Minds.—Led Zeppelin.—No one really. They were the most common answers. They failed."

In its finished state, the band, named The Commitments, consists of a pianist, guitarist, bassist, saxophonist, trumpeter, drummer, and lead vocalist, with three female backing singers, The Commitmentettes. Its manager is Jimmy Rabbitte. They perform old hits, mainly Motown, and these go down well at their first live gig, in a church hall. But what really gets the audience of 33 going is their version of "Night Train". To the stops name-checked in James Brown's original—Miami, Atlanta, Raleigh, Washington, D.C., Baltimore, Philadelphia, New York City, New Orleans—the lead singer adds local stations in and around the Irish capital, thus turning Soul into Dublin Soul.

There is plenty here that might be unfamiliar to non-Irish readers born after 1970: the '60s hits and their extensively quoted lyrics, some dialect words, and above all the fact that most of the book is local slang dialogue – there's very little description. But the narrative drive is so strong that these are scarcely noticeable bumps in a train ride that takes the reader through the heart of working-class Dublin, both geographically and spiritually.

ALONG THE SAME LINES

The stations in The Commitments' version of "Night Train" are listed in order eastbound from the city center on the DART, the Dublin Area Rapid Transit system: Connolly, Killester, Harmonstown, Raheny, Kilbarrack, Howth Junction, Bayside, Sutton. There's a frequent daily service and the current fastest journey time along this route is 24 minutes.

VIENNA PASSION

AFTER THE CIRCUS

MY BRILLIANT FRIEND

CAPTAIN CORELLI'S MANDOLIN

CHAPTER 2

EUROPE

THE CITY AND THE MOUNTAINS (1901)

JOSÉ MARIA DE EÇA DE QUEIROZ

On the rare occasions that José Maria de Eça de Queiroz (1845–1900) gets mentioned in the English-speaking world, he is generally referred to as "the Portuguese Dickens." This label is scarcely adequate for a writer who, in addition to being a social realist, was a modernist who covered explicit sex in *The Sin of Father Amaro* (1875) and *Cousin Bazilio* (1878). The latter is a work that, if more widely known, might rank with the three most widely acclaimed European novels of adultery: *Madame Bovary* (Gustave Flaubert, 1857),

Anna Karenina (Leo Tolstoy, 1878), and *Effi Briest* (Theodor Fontane, 1895). By the end of his life Eça had adopted an amused *fin de siècle* detachment about the human condition that is more like the Oscar Wilde of *The Picture of Dorian Gray* (1890).

Eça's late-stage insouciance abounds in this posthumous work, which chronicles the life of one Portuguese nobleman, Jacinto, as seen through the eyes of another, his friend Zé Fernandes, the narrator. Jacinto is living in the 1890s in a mansion on the Champs-Élysées in Paris (the city in which Eça lived for the last 12 years of his life), where his family has been exiled since the Portuguese Civil War (1828–34). With nothing pressing to fill his time, he tries to make himself the living embodiment of the philosophical notion that Man can be perfectly happy only when he is perfectly civilized.

Zé is then summoned home to look after his family farm in Guiães, Portugal. When he returns to Paris seven years later, he finds Jacinto surrounded by tens of thousands of books, most of them unread, and every conceivable modern convenience. There is even an elevator in which a divan, a bearskin rug, books, and cigars have been installed to ward off boredom on the seven-second journey between two floors. Since Zé was last there, Jacinto has acquired all the trappings of civilization but none of the bliss they're supposed to bring. He is, in short, suffering from "a surfeit of Paris."

PILGRIMAGE TRAIL

Start on the Atlantic coast in Eça's birthplace, Póvoa de Varzim, an attractive beach resort. There's a statue of the author in the main square, Praça do Almada. From Póvoa de Varzim take the A7 eastward and the A11 southeastward, parallel to and sometimes alongside the River Douro, to Fundação Eça de Queiroz and the Casa de Tormes, the house that belonged to Eça's wife and was the inspiration for the Portuguese setting of the book. Continue eastward, via the N108 and N222, to the village of Guiães, home of Zé Fernandes. The route runs roughly parallel to the River Douro and at times alongside it. The total distance is about 100 miles (160km).

Tired of having everything, and suddenly motivated by the desire to oversee the re-interment of his ancestors' remains, Jacinto decides to pay his first-ever visit to his ancestral Portugal. On his arrival there, with Zé, Jacinto's expectations that the countryside will be vastly inferior to the French metropolis are soon confounded. He falls in love with the mountains and throws himself into rural life with a greater enthusiasm than he ever displayed for the city. Jacinto comes to love "the sheer beauty of simplicity" and "the majestic way in which Nature falls asleep." Contented, he utters "a sigh like that of someone who can at last rest."

BELOW *Póvoa de Varzim has been a beach resort since long before Eça's birth here. Although its population has more than quadrupled since then, parts of the city are still as they were in Eça's time.*

FOR WHOM THE BELL TOLLS (1940)

ERNEST HEMINGWAY

The hero of this novel, Robert Jordan, an American, has left his job as a college teacher in Madrid to fight for the Republicans in the Spanish Civil War (1936–9). Dispatched behind enemy lines in Segovia province, northwest of the capital, he is tasked to blow up a bridge.

So that's one of the main themes: war. Another theme is rapidly established: love. Asked by one of his new guerrilla comrades about his personal life, Robert Jordan declares, "I have enough to think about without girls"—about as clear a sign as there can be in literature that the speaker will soon be romantically involved, in this case with Maria, who was raped by Fascist soldiers before finding refuge with the other side.

A third theme is intimated in the book's title, a quotation from a prose work by John Donne, best known as a metaphysical poet. The bell that tolls is the death knell; it may ring for someone else today, but sooner or later it will be your name on the clapper. And that's how it pans out for Robert Jordan, but not before he has made sure that Maria reaches safety and he has refused an opportunity to take the easy way out (that's another theme: the nature of heroism).

When *For Whom the Bell Tolls* was first published, the reputation of Ernest Hemingway (1899–1961) was firmly established and his stock rapidly rising. *The New York Times* judged the work "tremendous" and his "finest novel." The reviewer made special mention of the dialogue, "handled as though in translation from the Spanish," and described it as "incomparable." Whether this was a veiled criticism is unclear—the rest of the article is glowing praise—but to modern eyes the discussions between the characters seem so stilted that they prompt the thought that "incomparable" may be meant in the sense of "incomparably contrived." Examples abound throughout: the use of "thee" and "thou" in an effort to preserve in translation the distinction in Spanish between the formal "*usted*" and the familiar "*tu*"; the English rendition of a Spanish oath as "I obscenity in the milk"; and, returning to the love theme, the justly derided "Did thee feel the earth move?"

But what is timeless about *For Whom the Bell Tolls* is its evocation of Spanish terrain, which remains charming even when described in militaristic terms by an irregular soldier who is planning to destroy it.

Even in periods of conflict and in poor, oppressed areas, the literary image of Spain is above all romantic. Who better to capture this spirit in prose than Hemingway, an author whose machismo was to a large extent a cover for deep-rooted sentimentality?

ABOVE *Segovia sits atop a limestone ridge between two rivers, the Clamores and the Eresma. Hemingway's visit to the city may have inspired his description in* For Whom the Bell Tolls *of a town "built on the high bank above the river" with a central plaza, on three sides of which is "the arcade and on the fourth side is the walk shaded by the trees beside the edge of the cliff with, far below, the river."*

THE SHADOW OF THE WIND (2001)

CARLOS RUIZ ZAFÓN

In 1940s' Barcelona, 10-year-old Daniel Sempere, mourning the death of his mother, is taken by his bookseller father to the Cemetery of Forgotten Books, an enchanted place in which thousands of volumes wait for someone to choose them, whereupon they become a part of that person's life forever. Attracted by its binding—gold lettering on wine-colored leather—Daniel chooses *The Shadow of the Wind* by Julián Carax.

The rest of the story concerns the mysteries surrounding this work and its author. Daniel has the sole surviving copy of the book, and the author is supposed to have been killed in the Spanish Civil War (1936–9).

As Daniel grows up, he becomes increasingly preoccupied with his search for the truth. What happened to the rest of the print run? Who exactly was Carax? As he pursues it, he himself is tailed by a sinister figure who stinks of burned paper.

BELOW *The first stop for most visitors to Barcelona: La Rambla, the street that extends for three-quarters of a mile (1.2km) between the port and the Plaça de Catalunya.*

Meanwhile events in Daniel's life increasingly and worryingly seem to repeat those in the life of Carax.

To summarize the plot in greater detail would require more space than is available here and spoil the fun for those who have yet to read the book, which is a largely successful synthesis of *Bildungsroman*, love story, murder mystery, and thriller with an admixture of magical realism. The work is a global phenomenon: 40 different language editions, with approaching 20 million copies sold to date. Translated into English in 2004, it was the first in a quartet of books known as the Cemetery of Forgotten Books.

What Ernest Hemingway did for rural Spain, Carlos Ruiz Zafón (b. 1964) here does for the nation's second-largest and most cosmopolitan city. Stylistically, however, the two novelists could hardly be more different. Hemingway is perhaps best known for minimizing—almost eradicating—the adjectives that had proliferated in the novels of the generation that preceded him, and many of the words that he banished seem to have taken refuge in *The Shadow of the Wind*, in which the few nouns without epithets stick out like (rocky?) promontories or (sore?) thumbs. Some readers find these additional words a hindrance, but most think they enrich the texture of the narrative.

Apart from this criticism, which is, of course, a matter of personal preference, the main generally acknowledged flaw in *The Shadow of the Wind* is its ending. But endings are the weakest parts of most novels, and the plot of this one is so intricate that it would seem churlish to reproach the author for a creditable if flawed attempt to tie up his loose ends.

The success of *The Shadow of the Wind* has spawned walking tours through Barcelona that take in not only the real places that appear in the book but also some of the imaginary ones: Las

ABOVE *This tapas bar in Carrer de Montcada has two claims to fame: the sparkling wine from which it takes its name and its proximity to the Picasso Museum.*

Ramblas; the Arco del Teatro, near the fictional library/graveyard; Carrer de Montcada; the Santa Lucia Asylum; El Xampanyet tapas bar; Els Quatre Gats restaurant; Sempere and Sons bookshop and the family home; and the old library of Ateneu Barcelonès,

There are plenty of books set in the Catalan capital, but possibly none that so perfectly captures the past and present of the city while simultaneously contributing to its already rich mythology.

BIRDSONG (1993)

SEBASTIAN FAULKS

For anyone contemplating a trip around the World War 1 battlefields in the French part of Flanders, it is hard to imagine a better companion than this novel. Sebastian Faulks (b. 1953) opens with a vivid and accurate evocation of the regional capital Amiens, with its grand cathedral square and "gabled houses leaning over cobbled streets above the canals." Later he describes the straight, flat road to Bapaume, alongside which the great Thiepval war memorial looks "as though the Pantheon or the Arc de Triomphe had been dumped in a meadow."

Birdsong is rich in historical context, and the finest sections describe the first day of the Battle of the Somme in 1916 and the Battle of Messines in 1917. The gruesome and affecting details capture the way in which the carnage was so great and indiscriminate that it desensitized the combatants.

Divided into seven parts, the story spans three periods—before, during, and after World War 1—and the same number of generations. In 1910, a young Englishman goes to live and work in Flanders and there falls in love with a French mill-owner's wife. The two elope to Provence. So ends Part One.

In Part Two, the same young Englishman serves as an infantry officer in the British army. Among his comrades-in-arms is a Royal Engineer whose duty is to tunnel beneath enemy lines.

Part Three is set in England in 1978. A middle-aged woman develops an interest in her family history. Rooting around in her attic she finds a stack of her grandfather's diaries. That these journals are written in code has a double significance: within the context of the story, they reflect the deeply ingrained reluctance of people of the period to lay bare their deepest feelings. There is also a symbolic meaning: the code may be taken as a reference to the difficulty of recreating the past, of getting an accurate sense of what it was like to have lived in any era other than one's own.

This woman, who turns out to be the grandchild of the young couple to whom we were introduced in Part One, then visits the World War 1 battle sites in northern France and Belgium. She is appalled by the vast extent of the slaughter.

MESSINES RIDGE TOURS

The Battle of Messines was fought in June 1917 on the outskirts of the Flemish city of Ypres. Among the relics of this engagement are some of the tunnels dug by soldiers on both sides and a mine crater, 250ft (75m) across and 40ft (12m) deep, now filled with water and known as the Pool of Peace. Also within easy reach from here by car or bus tour are the German trenches at Bayernwald, the Australian War Memorial, the Island of Ireland Peace Park, and the St Eloi craters.

Part Four goes back to France in 1917, Part Five is set in England in 1978–9, Part Six takes place in France in 1918, and Part Seven is set in 1979 England.

Birdsong is by no means perfect. The reader may find it difficult to believe that the granddaughter knew so little about World War 1 before she began her research—she wonders if all traces of the conflict will by now have been "tidied away"—and credibility is further stretched by her exclamation when she sees the scale of what remains: "Nobody told me… My God, nobody told me." Nevertheless, few, if any, people who have seen Flanders fields have failed to be awed by the vast number of war graves and the funerary inscriptions in honor of those whose bodies were never recovered. And despite *Birdsong*'s overall structural flaws, the middle section does help the reader to imagine what it must have been like in the trenches, and to that extent it succeeds in deciphering history.

SOMME TOURS

The Battle of the Somme lasted from July 1 to November 18, 1916. Of the three million who fought in it, more than one million were killed. The result was inconclusive. The following are among the most important—and most affecting—local sites and memorials to what is now widely regarded as one of the most futile engagements in military history.

Serre Road Cemetery No. 2: More than 7,000 British graves, almost half of them unknown soldiers

Newfoundland Memorial Park: Preserved trenches of both sides

The Ulster Tower: Northern Ireland's national war memorial

The Thiepval Memorial: Designed by Sir Edwin Lutyens; the largest British monument to the fallen

The Lochnagar Mine Crater: Created by a bomb planted by the Royal Engineers and detonated on the first day of the Battle; roughly 330ft (100m) across and 98ft (30m) deep

AFTER THE CIRCUS (1992)

PATRICK MODIANO

This is a mystery and a thriller of a highly unusual and refreshing kind. Much fiction—indeed, much narrative art—is part set-up and part pay-off. Such skeletons may be fleshed out with backstories, dialogue, interior monologues, subplots, minor characters, and descriptions of indeterminate length, all of which may have a direct bearing on the plot but which may equally be discursive, or even rambling.

French author Patrick Modiano (b. 1945) strips away most of this paraphernalia. In Paris during the 1960s, a boy is quizzed by the police for no reason that he ever discovers; all they tell him is that they found his name in someone's address book. As he's leaving the interview room, he passes an attractive woman on her way in. He waits in a café across the road until she comes out, and then he hails her, introduces himself, and asks her what they wanted

her for. She seems to have no idea either. They go back to his place and sleep together.

All we know at this stage is that he's below the age of consent, and that she's a few years older. Nor do we find out a lot more about them later, other than that she is or has been married. She calls herself Gisèle; it's not until near the end that we discover that his forename is Jean.

These and other uncertainties create an atmosphere of suspense. An added sense of jeopardy derives from Gisèle's flightiness, her constant air of one who's about to go off for a few minutes and never come back. Fear that she might do so inhibits the boy from questioning her about her past; on one occasion when he does pluck up the courage, he finds her reply "at once too extensive and incomplete, as if she were trying to bury the truth under a wealth of detail." He pushes no farther because he's in love with her.

In the pivotal event (the peripety, after which in conventional novels exposition turns to dénouement) the couple is paid to do something that almost anyone might have done for free but which seems—only seems—to have made them accessories to a crime.

Finally, just as the answers to some of these questions may perhaps be discerned on the horizon, a sudden, shocking ending brings all lines of inquiry to a screeching halt. In other hands, the absence of a resolution might be frustrating, but Modiano's prose is like the cigarette in Oscar Wilde's *The Picture of Dorian Gray*: "Exquisite, and it leaves one unsatisfied. What more can one want?"

NAME DROPPING

"The city of Paris plays a central role in his writing"—this quotation is an extract from the award citation when Patrick Modiano won the 2014 Nobel Prize in Literature. *After the Circus* may make readers turn to a street map on which to follow the characters' journeys around the French capital. The places are all enumerated, if not actually described, in Modiano's minimalist style that creates an evocative atmosphere of menace: Pont Saint-Michel, Place du Châtelet, Avenue de la Grande-Armée, Boulevard Haussmann, Rue François Miron, Avenue des Champs-Élysées, Rue Washington, Rue Charles Dickens, Rue du Dragon…

LEFT *Pont Saint-Michel, over the River Seine—one of the Paris landmarks underpinning the story arc as the couple moves around the city.*

FRANCE

CHOCOLAT (1999)

JOANNE HARRIS

One of the narrators, Vianne Rocher, accompanied by her six-year-old daughter, Anouk, takes over a disused bakery in a village in southwestern France and turns it overnight into a chocolate shop. The premises stand just opposite the church, and they open in their new guise at the start of Lent, the season of abstinence in the Christian faith. This strikes the other narrator, Francis Reynaud, the local priest, as at least a challenge to his authority and at worst flagrant blasphemy. He's right to be suspicious, because Vianne Rocher is a witch.

However, rather than pyrotechnic wizardry, her supernatural powers take the form of psychological insights—she has a reliable sense of what people desire. Vianne's sorcery is based on intuition rather than hocus-pocus, but it's no less powerful for that. *Chocolat* is magical realism plus real magic.

The village setting is described in the opening pages as "no more than a blip on the fast road between Toulouse and Bordeaux." But it turns out to be one of those blips that many seem to notice: in 2012 the book's author, Joanne Harris (b. 1964), expressed surprise in *The Independent* newspaper that "lots of people have told me they've been to Lansquenet-sous-Tannes; they're convinced they've found it, and that they've been to the chocolate shop. One woman even wrote to say she had her wedding there." Why surprise? Because Lansquenet-sous-Tannes is the author's invention; there is no such place.

That it seems real is a tribute to imagination—mainly Harris's, but also that of the people who think they've been there. Certainly there are plenty of places in southern Aquitaine and the Gers department of the Occitanie region that may have provided some of the raw material for Harris's village and that now, in turn, aspire to be locations in her fable. Harris has hinted that she based Lansquenet-sous-Tannes on one particular village, but she has never said which one. Naturally there is plenty of speculation, and the place with the shortest odds is Nérac, which is well worth seeing even if it's not the one she had in mind.

SOURCE OF THE RIVER

Like Lansquenet, the Tannes river on which the village supposedly stands is fictional, but since it's described as a tributary of the Garonne, there are more than 20 such waterways on which it may be based. Among the leading candidates are the Ariège, the Arize, the Arrats, the Baïse, the Ciron, the Gers, the Louge, the Neste, the Save, and the Touch. The small towns that line these rivers may not be Lansquenet, but each has its own spell to cast.

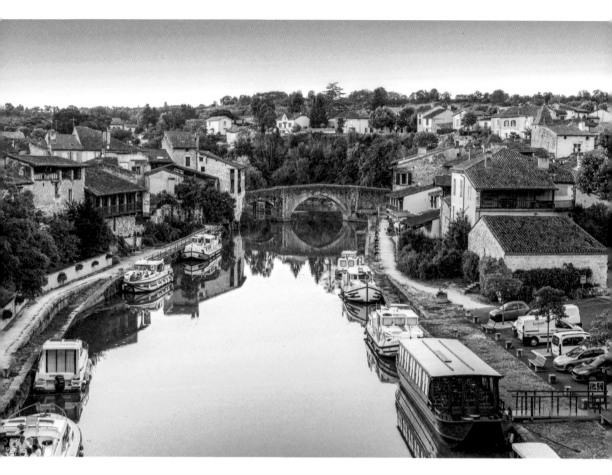

ABOVE *In an idyllic setting on the River Baïse, a left tributary of the Garonne, Nérac is one of several towns that may or may not be Lansquenet.*

UNCONSCIOUS ALLUSION

In a 2018 interview, Harris remarked that the name "Vianne," which she thought she had coined, was in fact the name of a village near the one on which she based Lansquenet. While she was writing she never realized. This is less of a clue to the whereabouts of the model than it seems: there are plenty of candidates in the vicinity.

A WIDOW FOR ONE YEAR (1998)

JOHN IRVING

We're more than halfway into this novel of 600+ pages when we learn the significance of the title, and we're even further into it when the American heroine reaches Amsterdam. But it's a stopover worth waiting for: what a vivid portrayal of the city it is, particularly the part of it that most tourists see almost immediately on arrival—the red-light district.

This section that evokes the vibrant spirit of the Dutch capital is only one of the pleasures of a great rambling novel in which there is almost no character without an interesting and well-told backstory (and it often is a story: most of those depicted are either practicing writers or fantasists who have reconstructed their histories in order to subjugate or cope with reality).

The plot in outline is as follows: Ruth Cole (aged four when we first encounter her) had two older brothers who were killed in a road accident before she was born. Tormented by the tragedy, her parents, Ted and Marion, are close to splitting up when the father hires a teenager, Eddie O'Hare, to assist him with his work over the summer vacation. For a while Eddie and Marion become lovers. At the end of the first part of the book, the mother goes off on her own, leaving the father to bring up the little girl.

A father who likes younger women breeds a daughter who likes older men: although the Electra complex never gets a name-check here (there's no cheap psychologizing), something like it is constantly in the background. The tension between Ruth and her father that constantly bubbles beneath the surface erupts more than once, most memorably during a game of squash.

There's also a murder, but that comes later; no spoilers here. Center stage throughout is the theme of writers writing, and the ways in which they mediate, mold, and sometimes subvert or duck reality. The Lothario father is a successful

SLOPING AWAY

That *A Widow for One Year* is the work of a writer at the height of his powers is demonstrated by the confidence with which Irving (b.1942) foreshadows subsequent revelations and comments on what his characters didn't know at the time but were destined to find out—two devices that ease the reader's path through a long, complex, multi-character tale.

As we are told, "A novel is always more complicated than it seems at the beginning. Indeed a novel *should be* more complicated than it seems at the beginning."

How odd, then, that the unfailingly assured narrative should be sprinkled throughout with italics like those in the above quotation: they're not obtrusive, but they're noticeable. Do we *really need* them?

author and illustrator of children's books. The daughter, the mother, and her one-time lover all become novelists: Ruth a celebrated one, the other two making something like a living. There's also plenty of interesting material about the day-to-day business of being a writer—public readings, signing sessions, the Frankfurt Book Fair, and some of the unjust criticisms that writers who face their public have to deal with.

THE MINIATURIST (2014)

JESSIE BURTON

Petronella ("Nella") Oortman gets married off at the age of 18 to Johannes Brandt, a much older Dutch businessman, and moves from her childhood home in the provincial town of Assendelft to live with him, his sister, and their servants in his opulent Amsterdam residence. He pays her no attention on their wedding night and little more thereafter, but he does give her an ornate dollhouse that is a faithful scale replica of their marital home. Nella spends much of her time acquiring tiny fixtures, fittings, and figures for it; her supplier is the mysterious miniaturist, or model-maker, of the title.

Set in late 17th-century Amsterdam, during the Dutch Golden Age, *The Miniaturist* is the debut novel of the English author Jessie Burton (b. 1982). Although the novel is not biographical—the story is entirely fictional—its most obvious inspiration is an elaborate cabinet dollhouse displayed in Amsterdam's Rijksmuseum. The dollhouse was once owned by the real-life Petronella Oortman, a rich 17th-century Dutch widow who had been married to a merchant named Johannes Brandt.

But more than that, there is a strong sense that Jessie Burton's imagination was fired by Amsterdam itself. Of course, the city today differs substantially from the late 17th-century setting described in the novel. Gone, among other things, are "the sea-smell, the masts of the tall ships in the middle distance." Also departed is the draconian legal code that operated in the Netherlands under Renaissance Puritanism; it has been replaced by a social liberalism that is widely caricatured as a laid-back attitude to almost everything. However, most of the buildings along the canals are largely unchanged, and the main action of this novel takes place on the Golden Bend of the Herengracht, which is still substantially as it was more than three centuries ago. The canals feature prominently throughout the novel: they smell rank in the summer, freeze over in the winter, and give up their secrets—including dead bodies—in the spring.

Among the book's other important locations that may still be seen are the Old Church at Oudekerksplein 23, now in the heart of the red-light district, and East India House at Kloveniersburgwal 48, which was built in 1606 and is now used by the University of Amsterdam. Just around the corner, at Old Hoogstraat 22, is another tourist attraction (though it was built c. 1738, therefore postdating the story), the smallest house in Amsterdam at 6ft 8in (2m) wide and 16ft 5in (5m) deep. Central Amsterdam is a compact area, so these buildings can be visited on foot in less than an hour, and the tour can also take in Kalverstraat, site of the miniaturist's fictional workshop.

ABOVE *Petronella and her husband live on Herengracht, one of the three main canals built in the early 17th century as concentric semicircles around central Amsterdam; the other two are Keizersgracht and Prinsengracht.*

GOODBYE TO BERLIN (1939)

CHRISTOPHER ISHERWOOD

Berlin has changed in many ways since this book was written, but this novel partly disguised as memoir achieves the dual distinction of capturing both a moment in history and something of the timeless quality of the city in which it is set.

The work was inspired by the time that Christopher Isherwood (1904–86), spent as a young English language teacher in the German capital. In the book, the first-person narrator—also called Christopher Isherwood—encounters a wide range of people: native Berliners and others who have gravitated to the city in search of employment, sexual liberation, or both. The morals of many of the characters are highly dubious, partly through economic necessity, perhaps also partly as a consequence of their own preferences.

The most famous of Isherwood's creations is Sally Bowles, a 19-year-old English singer who has come to Berlin in the belief that it is a stop on the way to Hollywood stardom. But she is not massively talented and she reveals herself to be a poor judge of who will advance her career—she sleeps with almost every man she meets.

This vivid literary creation later took on a life of its own, inspiring first *I Am a Camera* (a 1951 play by John Van Druten; later a film directed by Henry Cornelius) and then *Cabaret*. With lyrics by Fred Ebb and music by John Kander, *Cabaret* was a 1966 stage musical that six years later was turned into a celebrated movie directed by Bob Fosse and starring Liza Minnelli, Joel Grey, and Michael York.

Among the other vivid characters in the novel is Otto Nowak, the young lover of a rich Englishman the author meets during a summer stay on Ruegen, an island in the Baltic Sea. Otto is a scrounger and a thief, but his faults are later explained to some extent when the narrator learns of his home life in the Berlin slums.

The moment in history was the rise of Hitler. There are early scenes in which individual Nazis are derided and routed, but their destructive power grows during the course of the action. Before the reader's eyes, blond thugs in comical uniforms go from being laughing-stocks to becoming serious

LEFT *After lodging in several unsatisfactory flats, Isherwood settled in an apartment in this building at Nollendorfstrasse 17, in the Schöneberg district of Berlin. He remained there from December 1930 until he left Germany in 1933.*

threats. Also recorded here are some of the attitudes that were common at the time, particularly anti-Semitism and some chilling false assumptions, such as that mental defects may be caused by "hereditary syphilis" (a condition that does not exist).

Goodbye to Berlin ends in early 1933 when the narrator returns to England, but the novel is buttressed by the reader's knowledge of what happened next. On January 30 of that year, Hitler became Chancellor of Germany; before long,

casual racism and specious ethnic theories would spawn World War 2 and the Final Solution.

Politically and economically, Berlin today could scarcely be less like the place depicted in this novel. Moreover, much of the city has been rebuilt since World War 2. But on the streets, in the shops and cafés, and in the surrounding countryside, the prewar essence of Berlin has somehow survived the Hitler years intact—Isherwood evokes the way it is as well as the way it was.

EVERY MAN DIES ALONE / ALONE IN BERLIN (1947)

HANS FALLADA

Rudolf Ditzen (1893–1947) was a drunken, drug-addicted German who killed a man in a duel and was at various times confined in mental institutions. Hans Fallada, the pen name Ditzen adopted, was one of the leading exponents of a realistic style of writing known as the New Objectivity. He was big in the 1930s, both in his own country and abroad in translation, but his decision not to flee the Nazis did his reputation no good at all. Putnam, who had published his prewar books in English, turned down his later submissions, and in 1987 the company's former managing director, James MacGibbon, wrote in the *London Review of Books* that "Fallada is forgotten."

At the time he was right, but that changed in a big way in 2009 with the first publication in English of Fallada's 1947 novel *Jeder stirbt für sich allein*, under the titles *Every Man Dies Alone* (US)

and *Alone in Berlin* (UK). The paperback sold half a million copies in its first year, and the work is now widely acclaimed as a definitive fictional account of German resistance to the Nazis. A film, *Alone in Berlin*, based on the book was released in 2016.

Not that everyone in the novel's Berlin tenement block is opposed to the Third Reich: the building houses all shades of opinion, from a terrified old Jewess to an enthusiastic 16-year-old member of the Hitler Youth and his two brothers in the SS. In between these extremes are a retired professor who loves only justice, and conmen, busybodies, snitches, and prostitutes who just want to get by, no matter how humiliating or dishonest survival might be. One flat is the home of Otto Quangel, a taciturn factory foreman, and his wife, Anna. Otto stands out from his co-workers by refusing to join the Nazi Party—he claims he's apolitical, although privately he thinks that the subscription fees are no more than an unwanted additional tax.

At the start of the book, the Quangels learn that their son has been killed in action during the 1940 invasion of France. In their grief, they are galvanized into an unusual form of resistance: they write anti-Nazi messages on postcards which they leave lying around in public places all over Berlin. The first one bears the legend, "Mother! The Führer has murdered my son!" The man who finds it exclaims to himself, "My God!… Who would write something like that? They must be crazy! It's their death-warrant, for sure."

And so indeed it is, but before they get caught, the Quangels produce and disseminate a total of 276 subversive messages. Naturally this attempt to mitigate their grief does nothing to weaken Hitler's grip on power. Their postcards create terrible dilemmas for those who find them. Will they be suspected of writing them? Should they

FROM THE EDGE

The novel is based on the true story of Otto and Elise Hampel, a working-class couple who left postcards with messages such as, "German people wake up!" and "Hitler's regime will bring us no peace!" around Berlin. The Hampels were tried by the People's Court and beheaded in April 1943. The locations in the novel are all real. For a short walk between two of the most important sites, start at Keibelstrasse, a side street off Alexanderplatz, where the seven-story prison used by the Gestapo is now a memorial, and head north along Greifswalder Strasse to the junction with Jablonskistrasse, where the Quangels lived at No. 55.

pass them on, ignore them, or hand them in to the authorities? Are they being watched as they read them? Under the Gestapo's reign of terror, no one trusts anyone—as it turns out, with justification.

LEFT One of the displays in the Topography of Terror, the permanent exhibition now in the former Gestapo headquarters in Berlin.

THE READER (1995)

BERNHARD SCHLINK

Set in the late 1950s in Germany—no specific location, although the unnamed place seems a lot like Heidelberg, which is where Bernhard Schlink (b. 1944) comes from—this short work captures something of the essence of the way the nation is perceived abroad, as well as perhaps the way some of its older citizens perceive it themselves.

Michael, the narrator, aged 15 at the start, has an affair with Hanna, a slightly mysterious older woman who works as a tram conductress until she suddenly disappears from her job and his life. The next time he sees her is in the dock of a courtroom where she is being tried for Nazi war crimes.

During the proceedings it emerges that in World War 2 Hanna had been working on the assembly line at a Siemens factory until she was offered promotion to foreman, whereupon she preferred to leave the manufacturer and join the SS. She ended up as a guard at an offshoot of Auschwitz and was one of those responsible for leaving a group of Jewish women to die in a burning church. Under cross-examination she seems to admit that she was in charge at the time and that she later wrote the report on the incident.

But has she really admitted these actions or merely failed to deny them? As Michael watches the proceedings from the public gallery he thinks back to some of the odd things that happened during his relationship with Hanna. Slowly he realizes that she made this otherwise unaccountable wartime career change for the same reason as she quit the job she had when they were lovers. It was to conceal her darkest secret—that she can neither read nor write. Hanna has a chance to admit this during her trial, but her pride seems to prevent her from doing so. This weakens her defense and gets her a whole life sentence. The book is thus a study of the big question that has preoccupied Germans since 1945: who is guilty and who (if anyone) is not?

Some readers have taken Hanna's illiteracy as a metaphor for the German people, unable to "read" the consequences of allowing Hitler into power. Is an illiterate character a sympathetic character? Is illiteracy an excuse for being an agent of the Final Solution? That these questions go unanswered is a shortcoming in the novel, but Michael also faces a moral dilemma: he can tell the court that Hanna couldn't possibly have written the incriminating report, but worries that doing so would deny her free will. Thus is created a philosophical hall of mirrors in which the possibilities for self-doubt and recrimination stretch to infinity. In that sense, *The Reader* occupies a position at the very core of postwar German literature—it is about doing the right thing.

FILM SUCCESS

A film of *The Reader*, directed by Stephen Daldry and with a screenplay by David Hare, was released in 2008. It starred Ralph Fiennes as the older Michael, and Kate Winslet as Hanna. Winslet won an Academy Award for Best Actress in the role, and the film was nominated for Best Picture.

HOTEL DU LAC (1984)

ANITA BROOKNER

Readers who crave thrills and spills and passion should not trouble themselves with this novel; similarly, international travelers in search of uncertainty and turmoil need not bother with Switzerland. But those who value elegance and tranquility will put the prose of Anita Brookner (1928–2016) and the general worldview and lifestyle of the Swiss among their high priorities.

Edith Hope, the protagonist of this gentle story, is "a writer of romantic fiction under a more thrusting name" who tells her literary agent that "the facts of life are too terrible to go into my kind of fiction." She has been advised by friends to take a short foreign break in order to get over an "unfortunate lapse," which turns out to have been her decision to call off her wedding. Edith heads to the shores of Lake Geneva, where she stays in the fictional establishment of the title and slowly reaches the conclusion that a solitary life is not necessarily a lonely life.

Her sojourn is enlivened by fellow guests. Among them are two rich Englishwomen, Iris Pusey and her daughter, Jennifer, who at first make Edith their project, because she seems lonely. Thus they unwittingly submit themselves to scrutiny by the novelist, who is discerning but not all-seeing and records her interim judgments and conclusions about all the people she meets in regular letters home to her unattainable true love.

Also staying at the Hotel du Lac is a Mr Neville, who proposes to Edith after only a few days, his stated reasons for this forwardness being that he needs a woman he can trust and his conviction that she is "desolate." Edith is under no illusions: she knows an inveterate womanizer when she sees one.

In the mornings Edith works in her room on her new novel, *Beneath the Visiting Moon*. The view from her window inspires an opening description of the Alpine scenery, with "... boats skimming on the lake, passengers at the landing stage, an open air market, the outline of the gaunt remains of a thirteenth-century castle, seams of white on the far mountains, and on the cheerful uplands to the south a rising backdrop of apple trees, the fruit sparkling with emblematic significance."

ELSEWHERE IN SWITZERLAND

Anita Brookner captures the Swiss stillness. Many other novelists use the nation's mountains and financial industry as backgrounds for action and intrigue. Examples include *Banner in the Sky* (1954) by James Ramsey Ullman; *The Eiger Sanction* (1972) by Trevanian (pen name of Rodney William Whitaker); and *The Sigma Protocol* (2001), the last novel written completely by Robert Ludlum. For a late 19th-century Alpine idyll, read *Heidi* (1881), the timeless children's classic by Johanna Spyri.

In the afternoons, she goes for walks along peaceful sandy paths under the autumn sun.

This is Switzerland: a cool, restful retreat, sound-proofed from the cacophony of the rest of partisan, competitive, and ceaselessly squabbling Europe.

ABOVE *One of the many pleasure boats that ply up and down and across Lake Geneva, the setting for Hotel du Lac.*

AUSTRIA

VIENNA PASSION (1999)

LILIAN FASCHINGER

Vienna Passion reveals the spirit of the Austrian capital—the good and the bad—perhaps more clearly than any other work of literature.

Readers of this novel divide roughly into two camps. Fans regard it as a rich, multi-textured work in which the *fin de siècle* of the 19th century is challengingly interwoven with the final years of the 20th. They generally have a high regard for postmodern metafiction like this, in which the multiple perspectives enable an ironic commentary and a blurring of fact and fiction. Non-admirers see the book as overlong, unnecessarily complicated, and too full of coincidence. On the whole, they do not appreciate postmodern literary devices such as unrealistic plots, fragmentation, and self-reference by the author.

Almost throughout her prolific oeuvre, Lilian Faschinger (b. 1950)—Austrian-born but a long-term resident of Paris—displays some of the classic symptoms of exile: a sense of loss and deracination mixed with unshakable memories of what inspired her to leave her native land in the first place. Here her writing about the cradle of psychoanalysis reveals something not unlike a love–hate relationship with the city.

The opening describes Josef Horvath, a sickly young man whose mother looked after his musical education much better than his physical well-being, with the consequence that he has grown up to become a hypochondriacal singing teacher.

Next we meet Magnolia, an aspiring singer. American, of partly Austrian heritage, she comes to Vienna to do some background study for the part of Anna Freud, Sigmund Freud's daughter, in a forthcoming Broadway musical. While staying with her Aunt Pia, Magnolia discovers a manuscript memoir by Rosa Havelka. Born out of wedlock, Rosa ran away from the convent to which she had been sent and then lived on the streets, until her sexual allure enabled her to rise in society and eventually become mistress to Rudolf, Crown Prince of Austria. After her royal lover's suicide in 1889 she murdered a rapist and was hanged for her crime. Rosa had a daughter who turns out to be Magnolia's great-grandmother: thus are interwoven two strands a hundred years apart.

Faschinger's descriptions of Vienna are more evocative than a guidebook and sometimes not a lot less detailed, as, for example, in the list of all the city-center cafés that were frequented by Franz Schubert in the early 1800s and were still in business in the 1990s. There is nastiness here, too, such as Pia's remark, on first meeting Magnolia, that her mixed-race niece is blacker than she had expected.

At the end of the book, history is not exactly repeating itself but it is reverberating down the ages: Magnolia, who hated Vienna when she first arrived there, now loves it and is pregnant by her music teacher…

This book may not be an easy read, but it is a rewarding one, not only for someone planning a first visit to Vienna, but also for anyone who has already experienced its disquieting quality

of being simultaneously the timeless city of Schubert and Freud; the top-rated city in 2018, for the ninth year running, of the Mercer Quality of Living survey of the world's best cities to live in; and the capital of a land that time may seem to have forgotten, where the far-right Freedom Party of Austria can command one-quarter of the national vote.

ABOVE *This traditional coffee house is the oldest on Vienna's Ringstrasse, having opened at the same time as the boulevard itself. At the turn of the century, when much of this book takes place, it became known as Café Schwarzenberg. With the original marble cladding and hammered-brass tables, it retains a* fin de siècle *flavor.*

THE LEOPARD (1958)

GIUSEPPE TOMASI DI LAMPEDUSA

This novel about one period of uncertainty—the Risorgimento (period of upheaval that led to the unification of Italy in 1861 and the official move of the capital from Florence to Rome 10 years later)—was written during another: the aftermath of World War 2, when Italy abandoned monarchy and became a republic. That the Risorgimento was resolved well before the book was written rather intensifies the melancholy and nostalgia that suffuse *The Leopard*. Whatever Giuseppe Tomasi di Lampedusa (1896–1957) privately believed, his work seems to suggest that past outcomes are no guide to future performance and that, Karl Marx's famous dictum notwithstanding, history cannot be relied on to repeat itself in any way whatever.

The protagonist of *The Leopard*, Don Fabrizio Corbera, is the latest in a line of feudal landowners in Sicily. His nickname "The Leopard" is derived from

LEFT *A black leopard marks the entrance to the Palazzo Filangeri-Cutò (now a small museum devoted to Lampedusa) in Santa Margherita di Belice.*

POSTHUMOUS RECOGNITION

Lampedusa tried to get *The Leopard* published, but the long-established Italian publishing houses rejected him. He died almost a year before his work was eventually brought out, in 1958, by Feltrinelli, the Milan-based company founded only four years previously, which had just published the first Western edition of Boris Pasternak's *Doctor Zhivago*. The credit for noticing the quality of Lampedusa's unsigned manuscript submission goes to Giorgio Bassani, an editor who would go on to write his own celebrated work of modern fiction, *The Garden of the Finzi-Continis* (1962). An acclaimed film, *The Leopard*, directed by Luchino Visconti, was released in 1963.

the animal on his family crest. Don Fabrizio observes with a world-weary eye the gradual transfer of political power from the old, complacent, and corrupt Bourbon dynasty to the young, energetic, and no less corrupt bourgeoisie. His sense of the immutability of human nature rubs up against his awareness of life's transience, a conflict that is intensified after his nephew tells him, "If we want things to stay as they are, things will have to change"—a seemingly casual remark that was really the watchword of the book and has become its most famous line.

As Lampedusa anticipated, Sicily has been greatly altered since his death. Yet it remains sufficiently the same that visitors can still view some of the places described in his masterpiece. In Palermo, one may stand in the Via Roma and look out on "the scorched slopes of Monte Pellegrino, scarred like the face of misery by eternal ravines," which remain just as they were during the Risorgimento.

Also in the island capital are two important locations in Lampedusa's own life: Palazzo Lampedusa (at Via Lampedusa 23), where he lived for the first 47 years of his life, and Palazzo Lanza

EARTH-SHAKING

In January 1968 a series of severe earthquakes badly damaged Santa Margherita di Belice. The Palazzo Filangeri-Cutò was flattened and lay in ruins for a generation but has since had its facade and grounds restored. Inside there is now a modest café and a small museum of Lampedusa memorabilia, including his typewriter, manuscripts of *The Leopard*, various foreign-language editions of the novel, family portraits, and old photographs of Santa Margherita.

Also worth visiting in the town is the Museum of Memory, which stands on the site of the Mother Church described in *The Leopard*. It displays various items salvaged from the rubble as well as further photographs of how the town and surrounding area looked before the disaster.

EARTH-SHRINKING

Santa Margherita di Belice is 47 miles (75km) from Palermo. Lampedusa tells us that in 1860 this journey took Don Fabrizio three days. When the author made the journey in the 1900s—half by train, half by horse-drawn carriage—it took him 12 hours. Today by car along the SS624 in normal driving conditions, it takes just over an hour.

Tomasi (at Via Butera 28), where he died, aged 60. Both were hit by Allied bombing in 1943 but have been renovated and turned into apartment buildings.

Some of the other locations in *The Leopard* are fictionalized but remain easily identifiable. Lampedusa wrote in a letter that Don Fabrizio's country estate in the fictional town of Donnafugata was based on Palazzo Filangeri-Cutò, a 17th-century palace in Santa Margherita di Belice that had belonged to Lampedusa's great-grandfather (upon whom he said Don Fabrizio was based), and where Lampedusa spent childhood summer vacations. This town is generally thought to be the inspiration for Donnafugata in the book, but the author once said in a letter that Donnafugata was based on the nearby town of Palma di Montechiaro.

MY BRILLIANT FRIEND (2012)

ELENA FERRANTE

This is the first part of the four-volume *Neapolitan Novels* sequence. The other three books in the series are *The Story of a New Name* (2013), *Those Who Leave and Those Who Stay (2014), and The Story of the Lost Child* (2015).

The tetralogy concerns the interlinked lives of Elena ("Lenù") Greco and Raffaella ("Lila") Cerullo, childhood friends from an impoverished part of Naples: their loves and losses, their rivalry and mutual support, their struggles as working-class women in a middle-class man's world.

WHO IS THE REAL ELENA FERRANTE?

Elena Ferrante is the pseudonym of a writer who avoids personal publicity, on the grounds that she wants her work to be judged exclusively in its own right. She once wrote to her editor, "I believe that books, once they are written, have no need of their authors. If they have something to say, they will sooner or later find readers; if not, they won't." However, the very mystery that surrounds Ferrante's true identity has created enormous international interest—perhaps even more than the usual rounds of readings, signings, and celebrity interviews would have inspired.

The works are so deeply embedded in their setting that Ferrante fans trace the steps of the two heroines across the edgy heart of the Italian city. Most conventional guidebooks direct tourists west from the Central Station, but to see the neighborhood in which the heroines were almost certainly raised, it's necessary to head first in the opposite direction—Ferrante does not name the district, but few doubt that it's the Rione Luzzatti, which lies on the north side of the tracks just outside the railway terminus. The quarter is rough: a housing estate in which, as Ferrante depicts it, there seem to be more deaths and injuries than in some war zones. From here the only way, socially, is up.

Start at the Sacra Famiglia dei Padri Giuseppini, a 15th-century church that was originally in central Naples but was later transported brick by brick to the Via Carlo Bussola, because the area needed a church and didn't have one. From there, go south along Via Emanuele Gianturco to the tunnel with three entrances: the roadway beneath the railway tracks down which Lila and Lenù went when they bunked off school.

From here, you can either carry on, as they did, to the sea, or retrace your steps to Via Taddeo da Sessa—the *stradone* (main road) of the tetralogy—and turn left along it, past some public gardens on the right and the station on the left. The *stradone* becomes the Corso Meridionale.

At the junction with Corso Novara, turn left and then right across the Piazza Garibaldi, at

the far end of which is Via Carbonara. Then go through the Porta Capuana and turn north into Via Sant'Antonio Abate. Here in the O' Buvero street market, all the colors, the pushing and shoving, and the dialect swearing that abound in the *Neapolitan Novels* are brought to vivid if exhausting life.

Farther west, you come to Via Tasso in the upmarket Chiaia district: when Lenù and Lila first venture there, the rich women they see seem to them to have "breathed another air" and "learned to walk on wisps of wind." Farther along in the same direction is the Piazza dei Martiri, site of the fictional upmarket boutique in which Lila's shoes are sold.

ABOVE *Part of the open-air market that runs the length of the Via Sant'Antonio Abate.*

CROATIA
ILLYRIAN SPRING (1935)
ANN BRIDGE

In *Illyrian Spring* by Ann Bridge (1889–1974), 40-something Grace Kilmichael takes a trip to southern Europe to clear her head. Her marriage is collapsing and she is at loggerheads with the youngest of her three grown-up children. She's a well-known painter who might have been even more famous if she hadn't devoted most of her energies to making a home for her faithless husband, a distinguished economist.

While traveling, she strikes up a friendship with a man half her age who wants to be a painter but whose family sees him as an architect. As their relationship develops aboard Adriatic steamers, they share their thoughts about a wide range of interests and concerns, both external and internal.

With its heroine who abandons her home and doesn't tell her family where she's going, *Illyrian Spring* was mildly scandalous on first publication. The book became unfashionable when the popularity of graphic descriptions of sex made the platonic love described in it seem dated, but the work was later taken up by feminists and reprinted by Virago in the UK. Daunt Books brought out the latest edition in 2012.

Although the work has been dismissed as a mere travelogue, there is much more to it than that. The greatest pleasures of Ann Bridge's writing are derived from her descriptions of art, architecture, cuisine, and—above all—scenery. She sets the bar high at the outset with an account of Venice that captures the spirit of the city without resort to the over-familiar. On reaching the east coast of the Adriatic, her prose becomes even more evocative. Here is the companions' first sighting of Split (then known as Spolato), the largest city in the Dalmatia region of Croatia:

"… a twinkle of lights showed ahead, low down by the water, but nothing else. And then, suddenly, a miracle happened. From above their heads the ship's searchlight sprang out, and drew up out of the darkness before them a picture of a town, as if some vast creative hand raised up a great painted canvas from the floor of the night."

Bridge describes Dalmatia as a region "no one had ever heard of and where nobody ever went." That is no longer the case: modern Croatia is one of the world's most successful emergent holiday destinations, and this book has helped to popularize it.

LEFT *The waterfront at Split. The city on the Adriatic Sea is sheltered by the islands of Šolta and Brăc.*

ALBANIA
A GIRL IN EXILE (2009)
ISMAIL KADARE

In Albania under Enver Hoxha's dictatorship (1944–84), those who fell foul of the authorities might be sent into internal exile for repeatedly extendable five-year terms. *A Girl in Exile*, by Ismail Kadare (b. 1936), concerns Linda, a young victim of this punishment, who has been banished along with her parents for, it seems, the crime of being middle class. Prevented from traveling to Tirana, Albania's capital, on pain of death or life imprisonment, Linda constructs an elaborate fantasy in which Rudian Stefa, a playwright whose work she admires, becomes in her mind the embodiment of the capital city that she dreams of but can never visit.

Her friend Migena attends the first night of the dramatist's latest play, and in the foyer after the performance gets him to inscribe a copy of one of his works: "For Linda B, a souvenir from the author."

Later, Migena makes contact with Rudian again, and the two begin an affair. Not long afterward, Rudian is pulled in for questioning by state investigators. He wonders what they want him for. He has recently hit Migena, and she may have denounced him for that (he has previously been compelled to make self-criticism for his hot temper). He has also suggested that she was a spy, which would go badly against him if she were. Or they might be going to give him trouble about his next play, the text of which is currently under review by the censors.

As it turns out, Linda has committed suicide and the authorities are trying to find out how she came to have a signed copy of one of Rudian's books: did they ever meet in person? Gradually the background is filled in. As Linda's desire to see the bright lights intensified, so, too, did her obsession with Rudian: "[Migena] had never known anyone to love, with such wild intensity, a city they had never seen… this is how you love cities that you have no hope of visiting, like Dante's Florence…"

In a sense, Rudian Stefa is more than a place-filler—he is a personification of Tirana, not only to Linda but also to the reader. Both the character and the city are smart, with a slight air of menace, but beguilingly attractive, especially on "unforgettable… evenings when the light of the moon and the fragrance of the lime trees grew stronger."

A FOOT IN EACH CAMP

Kadare lived and worked in his native land throughout the Hoxha regime, with which he had an ambivalent relationship: some of his books were feted, others banned. After the dictator's death in 1985, Kadare was at first optimistic but progress toward democratization was slow. Feeling threatened, the author fled in 1990 to France, where he claimed political asylum. He was later repeatedly offered the presidency of Albania as the country tried to accelerate its modernization and liberalization, but he consistently declined.

CAPTAIN CORELLI'S MANDOLIN (1994)

LOUIS DE BERNIÈRES

When the Fascist forces of Italy invade the Ionian island of Cephalonia in 1940, one of their artillery captains, Antonio Corelli, falls in love with Pelagia, daughter of Iannis, the physician in whose house he is billeted. Corelli is a poetic soul who woos Pelagia by playing the musical instrument of the title.

Later in the story comes an account of real-life war crimes committed after the fall of Mussolini, when the Italians quit Hitler's Axis and prepared to fight on the side of the Allies. Their desertion incensed the Germans, with whom they had shared the occupation of Greece. On Cephalonia, Nazi troops set upon the Italians, slaughtering thousands of them.

In the meantime, Pelagia's ex-fiancé, Mandras, becomes a communist partisan. He goes off to fight on the mainland, then returns to Cephalonia during the Greek Civil War (1946–9) intent on showing his former girlfriend that he now knows all about atrocities.

This is only a faint outline of an ambitious work that features many narrative voices, most of which are fictional but some of which, including that of Mussolini himself, are historical. The mode of discourse also varies: part of the book is written in the first person, some of it is in the third person, and some of it is interior monologue.

Among the many strengths of *Captain Corelli's Mandolin* is its evident delight in languages—the English in which it is written, as well as Greek, Italian, and German—and some of the ways in which the languages interact. Occasionally this verbal exuberance becomes overblown (Dr Iannis doesn't just pee in his garden, he nitrogenates his herbs) but that's a minor criticism.

More serious is the possible objection that the book traduces Cephalonia by failing to reflect the extent of the islanders' resistance to the occupation, and their sacrifices during it. In addition, for using mainly English-language source material, its British author, Louis de Bernières (b. 1954) has been reproached by those who regard the British as invaders themselves.

But even some of the Greeks who criticize de Bernières have a pragmatic acceptance that the novel (as well as the 2001 film starring Nicolas Cage and Penélope Cruz) has brought much-needed revenue to an island that has always lagged behind its neighbor Corfu as a tourist destination.

LEFT *On a promontory on the west coast of Cephalonia, Assos was originally built by the Venetians in the late 16th century as a fortress to repel invaders. After World War 2 it was used as a prison farm for political prisoners, and it is now a popular tourist attraction in the small holiday resort.*

GREECE

THE ISLAND (2005)

VICTORIA HISLOP

In this first novel from Victoria Hislop (b. 1959), Londoner Alexis is about to go on vacation to Crete with her boyfriend. She knows the maternal side of her family came from that island, but her mother has previously been reticent about their Greek antecedents. Now, however, she gives Alexis her blessing to ask around and satisfy her curiosity.

Alexis visits Plaka, a coastal village to the west of the capital, Heraklion. Gradually she pieces together the family history she has never been told. Her great-grandmother developed leprosy and was forced to move to Spinalonga, an islet just offshore, where sufferers from the disease were kept in isolation.

She left behind her husband and two daughters, Anna and Maria. Maria later contracted the same disease and was sent to the leper colony, but by then drugs had been developed that enabled her and all her fellow inmates to be treated, cured, and ultimately released. Meanwhile, Anna had an extramarital affair and gave birth to Sofia. Her husband took this badly and shot Anna dead, for which he was sent to prison. Maria married the doctor who rid her of her disease, and together they brought up Sofia. They didn't tell their adopted child about her true parentage until they thought she was old enough to understand.

Sofia was ashamed of the problems she had caused, and angry that those she had always believed to be her parents were, in fact, her aunt and uncle. Deciding that she had been lied to, she found an English boyfriend, married him, and settled in London. Sofia is Alexis's mother.

In many ways this is a typical "beach" novel—most likely to be read by people while they're on vacation. But that should not be taken to imply that it is sensationalized or perfunctory. Its broad canvas, saga-like plot, and leisurely pace permit evocative descriptions of local details that bring Greece to life on the page: everything from the ancient ruins to "the sticky rainbow of plastic strips that hung in the doorway of the village bar… an attempt to keep the flies out and the coolness in." Moreover, the insights into a disease that brought shame as well as disfigurement and death raise *The Island* above the run of the paper mill.

RIGHT *In the early 16th century, Spinalonga was carved out of the coast of Crete and turned into an island fortress by the Venetians. From 1903 to 1957 the island was home to a leper colony.*

THE TOWERS OF TREBIZOND (1956)

ROSE MACAULAY

This is a work of contradictions: it is superficially comic but with an underlying seriousness; pagan but Christian; wildly popular on first publication but generally—and perhaps unjustly—neglected today.

Prima facie, it is the tale of a trip from Istanbul to Trabzon (the modern name for historic Trebizond, a Turkish city on the Black Sea) undertaken by Laurie, who is the narrator, her Aunt Dot, and a pompous Anglican priest in the company of a misanthropic camel with "spiteful memories in its insane eyes."

The sights, sounds, and smells of Turkey are described so vividly that it is hard to imagine readers not wanting to go at once to see the country for themselves. Also writ large is the historical background: Troy, St Paul, the Fourth Crusade, the Ottoman Empire, the rule of Kemal Atatürk. There is throughout the book an infectious joy in the actual process of travel, which Rose Macaulay (1881–1958) described as "the chief end of life": plotting the route, attempts to learn the language of the destination country, frontier bureaucracy, the cashing of travelers' checks, foreign food, and more are all described with amused affection.

There is also a wealth of good advice for travelers anywhere at any time. Warned against extending her trip to Russia, on the grounds that Russians persecute Christians, Aunt Dot roundly replies, "If one started not condoning governments, one would have to give up travel altogether, and even remaining in Britain would be pretty difficult."

Another quotation highlights one of the key differences between natives and tourists. Macaulay describes how the Turks, like other nations, want to demonstrate their progress, how they have "got on since Atatürk," but, "What foreign visitors care about is the things that were there before they began to get on."

But *The Towers of Trebizond* is more than a sophisticated fictionalized travelogue. The narrator is a middle-aged woman in a long-term love affair with a married man (as Macaulay was herself). The guilt that may accompany such relationships fuels the reflective passages in the latter part of the novel and justifies dramatically the shocking ending.

There is also considerable discussion of the doctrinal differences between the various branches of Christianity, and some of these distinctions, though clearly expressed, may yet be unclear to non-theologians. Perhaps that is what has driven *The Towers of Trebizond* out of fashion. But there is much here of current topicality as well as abiding interest, not least the discussions of women's rights. The travelers are joined en route by a local feminist who is interested in Anglicanism as a means to liberate Turkish women; with characteristic frivolity, Aunt Dot suggests that emancipation and sexual equality can be achieved by the wider use of the bathing hat.

ABOVE Turkey's Greek Orthodox Sümela (or Soumela) monastery is a major tourist destination 32 miles (52km) south of Trabzon. Founded in AD 386, the monastery ceased functioning in the 1920s.

RIGHT Part of the ancient city walls of Trebizond (Trabzon).

SNOW (2002)

ORHAN PAMUK

This novel by Turkey's best-selling author and Nobel laureate, Orhan Pamuk (b. 1952), is set in the eastern Turkish city of Kars, on the high plateau of eastern Anatolia, where temperatures can be sub-zero even in July and August. Despite the climate, the place is much frequented by tourists, both as a stopping-off point en route to Ani (see box) and as a destination in its own right. Between 1828 and 1918, Kars was periodically under Tsarist rule, and thus developed architecturally into an attractive slice of Russia in the heart of Asia Minor.

There are many other influences here, too: Turkish, of course, along with Azeri, Kurdish, Turkmen—and, hauntingly, Armenian. Kars is near the Armenian border (closed since 1993), and intermittently through its history Kars was part of Armenia. In *Snow*, a local museum commemorating "the Armenian Massacre" surprises foreign visitors who find there an exhibition of atrocities against the Turks rather than by them.

This is just one of the political problems of modern Turkey that Pamuk tries to address. The Turkish protagonist, Kerim Alakusoglu, known as Ka, having gone into exile in West Germany after the 1980 military coup, returns 12 years later for a variety of reasons. He is planning to attend his mother's funeral, to renew acquaintance with a lost love of his youth, to report on upcoming local elections, and to write an article for a magazine about a "suicide epidemic" among the city's young women.

Ka discovers that during his absence his fellow leftists have lost influence to resurgent forces of Islam. Kurdish separatist activity is making the city jumpy—the secret police shadow Ka's movements, and almost everyone he meets is an informer.

ANI

This atmospheric ruined city, a medieval ghost city in Kars province, 28 miles (45km) east of Kars, stands on the Akhurian River, which here forms the border with Armenia.

Ani became an important stop on one of the Silk Roads in around the year 400. In the latter part of the 10th century, the king of Armenia moved his capital here from Kars. The city, which once had a population of 200,000, flourished for two centuries but was then subjected to repeated Mongol raids. In 1319 it was devastated by an earthquake, and east–west caravan traffic was diverted onto alternative routes.

Ani is now abandoned (the nearest modern settlement is the Turkish village of Ocakli) but the ruins—of magnificent medieval stone churches and city walls—are essential sights for any visitors to the area.

ABOVE *A cat in the snow in Sarikamis, a town in the province of Kars, of which Kars the city is the capital.*

One source of tension is the Turkish state's ban on the wearing of headscarves in secular institutions. It is this, together with oppressive and restrictive traditionalist male attitudes to women, that is thought to have inspired the suicides.

Ka, a member of the educated, Westernized middle class who has hardly ever set foot in a mosque, struggles at first to understand why anyone should care about another's choice of clothing. But he is shaken out of his indifference when he witnesses the murder of a civil servant for enforcing the headscarf ban. While Kars is paralyzed by heavy snowfall, some political activists take advantage of the closed roads to put on a dissident theatrical entertainment. This sparks a confused sequence of events culminating in several deaths. Ka is expelled from town.

ABOVE *A cat in the snow in Sarikamis, a town in the province of Kars, of which Kars the city is the capital.*

Ka's account breaks off here, and it is left to the narrator, a friend of his with the same name as the author, to fill in the gaps. The fact that mysteries remain seems entirely appropriate in a political environment in which many people are keen to preach but unwilling to listen.

This work and other novels by Pamuk, particularly *My Name Is Red* (1998), are important aids to understanding a nation that is under intense pressure from left and right and from East and West.

FORGOTTEN FIRE (2000)

ADAM BAGDASARIAN

That Armenia is less visited than it deserves to be is attributable to two main causes: its tourist infrastructure remains underdeveloped and its history is underreported and sometimes misrepresented.

Armenia, the cradle of one of Europe's oldest civilizations, is much smaller today than it was in previous centuries. In addition to its current territory, it occupied most of the land between the southern Black Sea coast and Iran until the 14th century; but by the start of the 20th century, most of its possessions had been divided between Russia and the Ottoman Empire. During World War 1 and its aftermath, the Ottomans and their successors, the Turks, persecuted the Armenians, a Christian minority in a majority Muslim country. Between 1915 and 1923, Armenian property was systematically appropriated and its rightful owners deported or massacred—the exact number of dead is unknown, but informed estimates put the total at up to 1.5 million. This was one of the earliest modern genocides and one of the least documented.

In *Forgotten Fire*, Adam Bagdasarian (b. 1954), an American of Armenian heritage, aims to draw attention to these atrocities in a story based on the tape-recorded memoirs of his great-uncle. The novel charts the life of Vahan Kenderian, the youngest son of a wealthy family, whose sheltered childhood is brought to an abrupt end in 1915 when Turkish soldiers take some of his relatives away and murder others before his eyes.

Vahan goes on the run, and much of the novel is a succession of nightmare scenarios in which running escapes lead to worse trouble. *Forgotten Fire* is marketed as a novel for young adults, but its appeal is wider-ranging than that. It has high pace throughout and mature insights that never slip into tub-thumping or mawkishness.

Of course, we know that the narrator will make it to freedom, but we can never guess by what route or method. In this regard, Bagdasarian starts off with an advantage over many other accounts of wartime struggles: because the Armenian genocide has previously been so little written about, predicting the detailed course of events is almost impossible. The author is consistently good at making the trustworthy appear shifty and the dishonest seem like models of rectitude.

It would be a mistake to visit Armenia without some knowledge of the tragedy that befell its people, and this book is a highly readable introduction to an event that remains raw in the tribal memory more than a century after it occurred.

LEFT *The Armenian Genocide Memorial Complex in Yerevan, Armenia, stands within view of Mount Ararat, the highest peak in Turkey.*

THE RUSSIAN DREAMBOOK OF COLOR AND FLIGHT (2009)

GINA OCHSNER

In this compelling work of magical realism by Gina Ochsner (b. 1970), communism is dead in Russia, but the nation's community is still alive and well.

The story features a bizarre group of neighbors in a decrepit apartment block in Perm. This city in the Urals was closed to foreigners throughout the Cold War but is now accessible to everyone, and is thus a microcosm of the gradual opening up of the whole of Russia after the fall of communism.

Each of the neighbors is a 1990s' Russian archetype: Yuri, a traumatized veteran of the Chechen War; Olga, a Jewish translator for a heavily censored newspaper; Azade, a widow from Dagestan; Zoya, an aspiring "New Russian" who dreams of bettering herself by acquiring "prestige toilet paper" and a toaster oven; Vitek, a would-be Mafia boss; and Tanya, who works at the All-Russia All-Cosmopolitan Museum of Art, Geology, and Anthropology, where the exhibits are all fake, and who dreams of becoming skinny enough to work for national airline Aeroflot. Meanwhile the ghost of Azade's husband, Mircha, haunts them all, and a pile of rubbish inexplicably and uncontrollably builds up around them.

Described in *Russian Life* magazine as "bouncing between farce, fable, and fantasy," the book keeps one foot firmly rooted in fact, while the other swings out to the fantastic in an entertaining but pointed way. Characters are well aware of the true mortality and birth-rate statistics, but either they obfuscate them by reporting only

the successful production of toy penguins rather than the casualties of war, or they ignore them by focusing on the fabrication of Russian Orthodox icons from bouillon cubes and hairspray.

With clouds that have "the look of buckwheat porridge" or that are "congealed like winter soups," and "herring-scaled" skies, the language of Ochsner's novel is evocative and decidedly Russian, although the author herself is American. There is a pervasive sense of empathy and understanding, despite the witty satire. As Tanya notes, "suffering—if done beautifully—is an art form."

The possibility of securing a grant for the museum from a group calling itself "Americans of Russian Extraction for the Causes of Beautification" brings the characters together to try to convince the visitors that their representation of Russian culture is worth investing in. Ultimately, however, the potential sponsors decide not to put money in to the museum because, Tanya realizes, they want "a museum that resembled those on postcards [...], a Russia that existed only in dreams."

The community's final destruction of Mircha's ghost and acceptance of its own reality, rather than that seen through the eyes of the Americans, suggests it may be able to launch into a bright new future on its own, slightly wacky, terms. This surreal and darkly comic story is also a powerful satire of post-Soviet Russia combined with a celebration of the heart of its people.

BACK TO MOSCOW (2016)

GUILLERMO ERADES

PhD student Martin's expat life in Russia is the subject of this debut novel from Guillermo Erades—who, though born in Spain, lived in Moscow in the early 2000s—but it is the city itself that is the real star.

Westerner Martin is attempting to investigate "the evolution of the female character in Russian literature" for his studies, but he soon neglects the books in favor of real-life experience of the *dyevs* (young Russian women) he picks up in the capital's numerous nightclubs. The bright lights and 24-hour thrills of Moscow hot spots Propaganda, Boarhouse, and the Hungry Duck are distracting and ultimately irresistible to a young man new to the city.

Martin's arrival in Russia at the start of the 21st century coincides with the beginning of the Putin era, a period of radical change and growing opportunity. Martin and his friends, fellow expats living lives of little work and lots of vodka, are rightly convinced that they are witnessing a crucial moment in history.

The title and introduction to each chapter make reference to heroines of Russian literature, but the analysis is not quite as deep as these names might make you think. The themes discussed do not run through the story, and the women Martin meets are not well enough developed to bear any convincing comparison to, say, Sonya Marmeladova from *Crime and Punishment* (1866) or Tolstoy's *Anna Karenina* (1877).

But Martin isn't deep either; and neither is Moscow in the early 2000s, especially not for an expat who lives a kind of half life, never quite affected by or affecting the city in which he lives. Martin is largely flippant and shallow, and he lives in a city where his main concern is overcoming "Face Control," the brief glance that Moscow nightclub bouncers give would-be patrons to

THE SUPERFLUOUS MAN

Martin's professor accuses him of being a modern version of the "superfluous man," a deliberate comparison that flips the hero's repeated literary references back on himself. The "superfluous man" is a mid-19th-century Russian literary concept: a person who may be talented and capable, but who is bored, unambitious, indifferent, and cynical and who prefers gambling, drinking, or chasing women to engaging with society in any meaningful way.

The term was popularized by Ivan Turgenev in his 1850 novella *The Diary of a Superfluous Man* and was retrospectively applied to many characters from Russian literature, including Pushkin's Evgeny Onegin in the novel of the same name (1825–32), Lermontov's Pechorin in *A Hero of Our Time* (1840), and Ilya Ilyich Oblomov in Goncharov's *Oblomov* (1859).

assess whether they are good-looking and rich enough to be granted entry.

We learn very little about Martin prior to his arrival in Moscow. Most of his past remains a mystery, while his life in Moscow is practically inconsequential, beyond being a lot of fun. Only the book's final act brings him up close and personal with an infamous moment in Russia's recent history—the 2002 Nord-Ost theater siege by Chechen separatists in which no fewer than 170 people were killed. But even this leaves him unscathed—it seems to be only the *dyevs* who suffer any consequences of the situation in their country.

Martin rejects the idea that writers, as Dostoevsky suggested of Pushkin, might be able to reveal "great and immortal embodiments of the Russian soul." But Martin is wrong—in *Back to Moscow*, Erades paints such an accurate picture, simultaneously alluring and repellent, of both the darkness and the light of life in Russia that he has gone some way to doing exactly that.

RUSSIA AT THE START OF THE THIRD MILLENNIUM

In the 2000s, Russia was in transition. The instability of Boris Yeltsin's years as President was largely over, and his successor, Vladimir Putin, vowed to crack down on the oligarchs who had wielded vast power in the 1990s. Before he was elected, Putin claimed that Russia was "part of European culture" and that he "would not rule out" the possibility of joining NATO. The poverty rate fell from 35 percent in 2001 to 10 percent in 2010, while the size of the middle class grew from 30 percent to 60 percent of the total population in the same period. Oil-fueled economic growth helped to boost living standards, and Putin's approval rating was over 70 percent for most of his first two presidential terms (2000–2008) and sometimes exceeded 80 percent.

FACELESS KILLERS (1991)

HENNING MANKELL

In this novel, Swedish crime writer Henning Mankell (1948–2015) began the process of turning a small real-life ferry port in southern Sweden into one of the fictional murder capitals of the world—a place in which the body count became comparable to that in the Oxford imagined by Colin Dexter in the Inspector Morse novels.

SCANDI SLAY CENTER

Before Wallander, for most non-Swedes, Ystad was a point on a route rather than a destination. Now it has a tourist infrastructure and offers guided tours featuring various places in the novels, including the police station, Wallander's home at Mariagatan 10, and some of his favorite eateries, such as Bröderna M pizzeria, the Hotel Continental (Hamngatan nos 11 and 13, respectively), and Fridolfs Konditori (Lingsgatan 3).

On the outskirts of the town, on the site of a former army compound, are Ystad Studios, set up by Mankell for the filming of the Wallander series and now a production center for other Scandi TV series such as *The Bridge*. The studio's visitor center is open to the public.

The town in question is Ystad, which is linked by a regular ferry service with Świnoujście, the port city of Szczecin, Poland. After the fall of the Berlin Wall in 1989, Ystad became the point of entry to the West for refugees from the communist bloc and farther afield. Sweden had an open-door policy for migrants but struggled to meet the demand for residence permits, so Skåne County, where Ystad is located, became the site of many refugee camps.

It is against this background of political upheaval and social change that Mankell's detective hero, Kurt Wallander, investigates the brutal—and at first apparently motiveless—murder of an elderly couple on their remote farm.

As a character Wallander is flawed and damaged but idealistic. He's overweight, he drinks too much (and drives under the influence of alcohol), he is soon to be divorced, and he has a daughter who has attempted suicide. He's been a policeman for more than 20 years and has learned to be philosophical about the ways of the world. Significantly, his watchword—"a time to live and a time to die"— is from Ecclesiastes, the cynic's bible-within-the-Bible. He deplores racism, plenty of which features in this book, but believes that his government's approach to immigration is not thought out and plays into the hands of the extreme right. At one point he demands exasperatedly, "People who belonged to the fascist secret police in Romania are starting to show up here in Sweden. Seeking asylum. Should it be granted to them?"

Faceless Killers was an international triumph. Mankell went on to produce 10 more Wallander novels as well as short stories and, finally, *Before the Frost* (2002), in which the investigation was led by Linda Wallander, who followed her father into the police force. There have also been both Swedish and British television adaptations, as well as Swedish films, of the novels.

ABOVE *Mariagatan 10 is a perfectly good-looking building, but it would not have found its way onto the tourist trail had it not been chosen by Mankell as the home of his detective hero.*

DEATH IN OSLO (2006)

ANNE HOLT

In January 2005, Helen Lardahl Bentley is inaugurated as the 44th President of the United States. She is the first woman to hold the office. Five months later she makes her first official overseas visit to the land of her ancestors, Norway. Bentley arrives on May 17, Norwegian Constitution Day, a national celebration, when there is much carousing and reveling in the streets. Within hours of her arrival in Oslo, she is kidnapped.

How she came to be spirited out of a heavily guarded hotel room becomes a major bone of contention between the security forces of the two nations that were supposed to be looking after her and are now looking *for* her. As the investigation proceeds, there are several scenes in which all-action Americans come up against stubborn Norwegians—stereotypes, perhaps, but amusing and credible ones in the context.

Death in Oslo is a fast-moving thriller with a lot of characters. Yet the Norwegian author (and former Minister of Justice), Anne Holt (b. 1958), keeps all the characters and plot strands clearly delineated, so there's no need to turn back the pages to recall who was previously doing what to whom.

One of the qualities of the novel is the way in which the reality of Norway plays against the folk memories of Norwegian–Americans who've no firsthand experience of the old country. Madam President is expecting the land of her ancestors to be "beautiful and frightening, with rugged mountains everywhere," as her grandmother (who'd never set foot in the place herself) had described it to her. But instead, Bentley's brief first impressions are that the terrain around the capital was "friendly, with rolling hills and mountains with snow on their north-facing slopes. The trees were starting to parade that luminous green colour that belonged to the time of year."

VIK AND STUBØ

Anne Holt is a prolific author. *Death in Oslo* is the third novel in a series featuring Norwegian detectives Johanne Vik and Adam Stubø: she is a former FBI profiler (the brains of the duo), and he is an Oslo police superintendent (the muscle). The previous titles were *Punishment* (2001) and *The Final Murder* (2004). Thus far there have been two further volumes in the series: *Fear Not* (2009) and *What Dark Clouds Hide* (2012).

When Johanne Vik needs advice, she turns to retired detective Hanne Wilhelmsen, who is herself the heroine of Holt's other series of novels, which to date runs to 10 titles, most recently *In Dust and Ashes* (2016).

LEFT *The annual Norwegian Constitution Day parade along Karl Johans Gate, one of the main streets in downtown Oslo.*

DENMARK/GREENLAND

SMILLA'S SENSE OF SNOW/MISS SMILLA'S FEELING FOR SNOW (1992)

PETER HØEG

The assertion that the Inuit have 50 words for snow is often repeated and, although it is now generally regarded as inaccurate, they do have a greatly heightened awareness of the processes that produce different forms of snow and ice, and many words to describe these variants. Among those noted in this novel are *apuhiniq* (frozen drifts), *pirhuk* (light snow), and *qanik* (big crystals).

Also significant to the Inuit are the marks that may appear on snow. It is this expertise that enables Smilla Jaspersen, the half-Danish, half-Inuit heroine of *Smilla's Sense of Snow* (US title)/*Miss Smilla's Feeling for Snow* (UK title) by the Danish writer Peter Høeg (b. 1957), to suspect foul play in the death of her six-year-old friend, Isaiah. She believes that he didn't fall off the roof of his block

of flats, as the Copenhagen authorities would have the record show, but was pursued to his death.

Smilla's search for the truth leads her from the local morgue in Copenhagen to Greenland, where she was born more than 30 years previously. As a child in the 1960s she was transported, like so many Inuits of her vintage, to Denmark, there to be deracinated and socially segregated in a poor part of Copenhagen. This background turned her into a maverick and a rebel, and she thus fits neatly into the august literary tradition of oddball sleuths—professional and amateur detectives with more psychological baggage than instruments of forensic analysis.

The mystery of Isaiah's death involves big business corruption, organized crime, neo-Nazis, mad scientists, and the mining of Greenland's cryolite, a mineral used in the extraction of aluminum from bauxite. The plot is complicated but Peter Høeg's account of the treatment of Greenlanders before and after their country was granted home rule in 1979 brought some previously little-known injustices to general attention. It also whetted the appetites of tourists for both the Danish capital and the world's largest island.

In Copenhagen, we encounter not only the famous sights—such as Strøget (one of the longest pedestrian streets in the world) and Kongens Nytorv (the large square at one end of Strøget)—

TO THE TOP OF THE WORLD

Currently, the only scheduled flights to Greenland are from Copenhagen and Reykjavik, with Air Greenland or Air Iceland. There are summer sea cruises from Iceland, and some transatlantic cruise liners stop off at the southern tip of the island en route between Europe and North America.

but also the docks, which Høeg makes attractive even before dawn in a deep and dark December:

"The jackhammers on Knippels Bridge. The traffic starting up. The seagulls. The distant bass sound, actually more like a deep vibration, of the first hydrofoil to Sweden. The short toots on the horn of the Bornholm ferry as it turns in front of Amalienborg Palace. It's almost morning."

Høeg's Greenland is no paradise—the country's suicide and homicide rates are among the highest in the world—but its natural wonders are evoked in a manner that may make the reader want to see them in case they're destroyed by industry and global warming.

MISS SMILLA EXPLAINS

"Reading snow is like listening to music. To describe what you've read is to try to explain music in writing."

BELOW *Copenhagen's Amalienborg Palace, home to the Danish royal family, in the foreground and, on the far side of a harbor inlet, the Copenhagen Opera House on the island of Holmen.*

A GRAIN OF WHEAT

A DRY WHITE SEASON

HALF OF A YELLOW SUN

SAVUSHUN: A NOVEL ABOUT
MODERN IRAN

CHAPTER 3

THE MIDDLE EAST
AND AFRICA

TO THE END OF THE LAND (2008)

DAVID GROSSMAN

Central to this complex novel is the walk across Israel from north to south, starting in Galilee, undertaken by a mother and the father of one of her children. That they never make it even as far as Jerusalem may be taken as symbolic in a novel that endeavors to cast light on a road with no visible ending. The Israeli author, David Grossman (b. 1954), captures, or at least momentarily reveals, something of the essence of the Arab–Israeli conflict—not only that between the two peoples but also the conflict within individual Jews—in all its bewildering and often dispiriting intractability.

The heroine, Ora, meets Ilan and Avram during the 1967 Six-Day War while they are patients in a fever hospital, and the three become friends. Ora later settles down with Ilan and they have a son, Adam. In the 1973 Yom Kippur War, Avram is captured and tortured by the Egyptians. He returns home traumatized by his experience. Ilan has meanwhile left Ora, so she moves in with Avram until she falls pregnant, whereupon he kicks her out. She gives birth to another son, Ofer; Ilan returns and he and Ora bring up both boys. Avram never sees his son, and has no contact with Ora for many years.

When the children reach the age of conscription, Adam does his time in the army and then heads off with his father on vacation to South America. Ofer stays on in uniform after the compulsory service

period and volunteers to take part in Israel's 2006 attack on Hezbollah Shi'as in Lebanon. Horrified by Ofer's choice, Ora finds Avram, now a near derelict, and drags him with her on her walk. She takes every possible precaution against receiving information from the outside world, thinking that as long as she keeps walking she cannot receive the news she dreads—that Ofer has been killed in action.

Ora and Avram walk part of the northern section of the Israel National Trail, a path that is roughly 680 miles (1,100km) long between Kibbutz Dan, near the Lebanon frontier at the foot of Mount Hermon, and Eilat, on the Gulf of Aqaba. The sights along their route are affectionately described, but the landmarks they pass most frequently are memorials to the dead from all the conflicts since the foundation of the state of Israel in 1948.

RIGHT *The Red Canyon is an easily accessible hiking trail near Eilat.*

EGYPT

THE CAIRO TRILOGY (1956–57)

NAGUIB MAHFOUZ

The titles of the three volumes of this saga—*Palace Walk* (1956), *Palace of Desire* (1957), and *Sugar Street* (also 1957)—are taken from the names of the real Cairo streets in which the principal characters spend their adult lives. The trilogy, by the Nobel laureate Naguib Mahfouz (1911–2006), who grew up in Cairo, covers the period between the last year of World War 1 and the last year of World War 2. The thoughts and actions of the al-Jawad family reflect and are influenced by contemporary political events in Egypt.

In the first volume we are introduced to the domestic set-up of a wealthy Cairo merchant. Ahmad Abd al-Jawad is an old-fashioned patriarch: sternly disciplinarian indoors and self-indulgent outside the home, drinking and womanizing to his heart's desire.

He is cruel to his wife, Amina, but she consoles herself with the thought that this is how real men are supposed to behave. Thus she is content with the restrictions he places on her movement. By the time her sons persuade her to visit a mosque during Ahmad's absence on business in Port Said, she has not been outside the house for a quarter of a century. When her husband learns what she has done, he punishes her for disobedience, but the streets of Cairo have been an epiphany for Amina. Life will never be the same for her again.

At the same time, big changes are happening in the world beyond the al-Jawad household: the start of the Revolution of 1919, when the Egyptians rose decisively against their British rulers. (Egypt went on to gain its independence in 1922, with the British maintaining control over foreign relations, the military, and other aspects until the Revolution of 1952, when the kingdom became a republic.)

The al-Jawad family consists of three sons and two daughters. The eldest boy, Yasin, is Ahmad's by a previous marriage; Yasin is dissolute, like his father. The middle son, Fahmy, is a sensitive youth who is hurt by the debauchery of his father and older half-sibling; he becomes active in the struggle against the British occupation. The youngest son, Kamal, is a thinker and a bit of a loner, who befriends the British soldiers guarding the street outside the family home, studies philosophy at university, and eventually becomes a teacher. The elder daughter, Khadija, is clever but physically unprepossessing, while the younger girl, Aisha, is beautiful but stupid. Aisha gets married first, and her wedding is the pivotal event in the first volume of *The Cairo Trilogy*. During the party, alcohol is consumed, tongues loosen, secrets are exposed, and some home truths get spoken.

There is much to be gleaned about the history of Egypt during the late-colonial period and under the current independent government. One of the strongest motifs in the work is faith. The Qur'an is quoted and referenced throughout by all the main characters, and questions of belief are never far from the surface. Mahfouz also captures the image of the nation's capital in all its teeming variety, where ancient and modern, opulence and grinding poverty, wisdom and ignorance, palaces and slums all assault the senses and bewitch residents and visitors alike.

THE RUINS OF US (2012)

KEIJA PARSSINEN

American Rosalie met Arab Abdullah while they were studying at university in the United States. He wooed her by declaiming the work of 20th-century Syrian poet Nizar Qabbani:

"When I love you, I march against ugliness, against the kings of salt, against the institution of the desert!"

Rosalie and Abdullah married and moved to his native Saudi Arabia, where he made a fortune in the family business. A quarter of a century and two children later she discovers that he's had a second wife for the past two years. She confronts him. He reminds her: "When you chose to marry me and move here, you told me that you were ready to accept my culture. You said you loved my culture. Well, this is my culture."

Rosalie points out that, even in the Gulf, polygyny is now a custom more honored in the breach than the observance. But Saudi Arabia is a man's world, and Abdullah is accustomed to getting his own way. In the ensuing domestic strife, the main victims are the couple's teenagers: Mariam, Western-inclined in her mother's likeness, who writes a sassy blog that can only get her into trouble with the local law; and Faisal, an observant Muslim who despises his father's drunkenness and comes close to being radicalized by an Islamist sheikh.

The rest of the story is not exactly happy, but disaster is averted by the stoicism that makes the best of a less than perfect job. Half a lifetime's shared experience, particularly parenthood, is finally more powerful than the spell cast by a young woman on an older man.

This is the debut novel from Keija Parssinen. Born in Saudi Arabia, she spent her first 12 years on a Saudi compound before moving with her parents to their original home in Texas—Rosalie's journey in reverse. The author's youthful experiences inform her portrait of the relentless heat, the desert, the sea: "a dhow whose wooden frame stabbed at the falling sun, or a low dune fully covered in purple flowers."

Parssinen also describes the lifestyles of Saudis and expatriates. The mall is the Saudi equivalent of the US bar: a place where boys and girls meet. Or at least they try to—young males, we learn, are "barred from entering the mall without family to reduce the threat that [they] would roam and flirt and disturb the order of things." Police are everywhere, insuring that no alcohol is around and no women drive cars. Americans watch *The Sopranos* on illegal satellite TV. On Thursday nights, the start of the Arab weekend, Western drivers create a rush hour as they line up to get over the frontier bridge to the island kingdom of Bahrain, where the drinking laws are not so strict and there's a much sought-after happy hour.

RIGHT *Al Faisaliah Mall in Riyadh, Saudi Arabia, is full of high-end retail outlets and restaurants.*

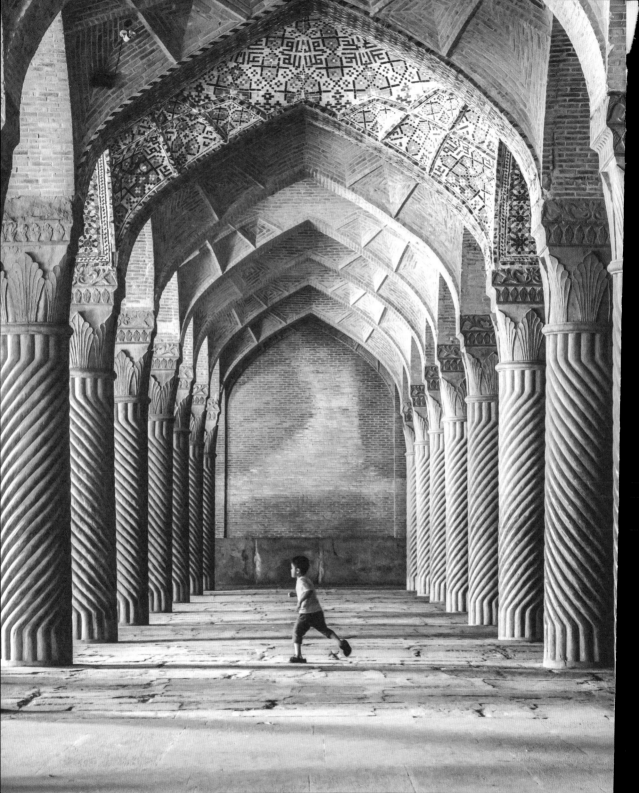

SAVUSHUN: A NOVEL ABOUT MODERN IRAN (1969)

SIMIN DANESHVAR

Written by academic and novelist Simin Daneshvar (1921–2012), *Savushun* (entitled *A Persian Requiem* in the 1992 translation) is the first novel in Persian by an Iranian woman. It is about love that both endures and is enduring and about exploitation in several of its forms, notably political and sexual. Its title refers to a traditional mourning custom that aims to keep hope alive in times of sorrow and adversity.

The action takes place during World War 2, when Iran is occupied by Allied forces and divided into three zones. The Soviet Union controls the north of the country, the United States holds the center, and Britain runs the south. Southern Iran includes the city of Shiraz, where Zari, the protagonist, lives with her husband, Yusof, a rich landowner, and their three children: a son, Khosrow, and twin daughters, Marjan and Mina.

Yusof is outraged by this latest in a long series of outside interventions in his country. He tells his compatriots, "There is nothing surprising and new about foreigners coming here uninvited… What I despise is the feeling of inferiority that has been instilled in all of you." Defiantly, he refuses to sell his grain to the British. When his brother Khan Kaka protests that "an army that big can't be kept hungry," he replies bitterly, "But my peasants and the people of my city can be…"

LEFT *The Vakil Mosque in Shiraz, the city where Zari and her family live, was built in the 18th century.*

Yusof's decision is the cause of all ensuing harm. As the storm clouds of tragedy gather, Zari holds the family together, devotedly obedient to her husband and constantly admiring of his principles, regardless of her private doubts about the wisdom of his actions.

She suffers in silence, but she cannot stop herself thinking. She theorizes that men are more competitive than women because they cannot give birth, and that those traits which are conventionally regarded as masculine—restless action, physical strength, the urge to finish first— are mere consolations for males' inability to create anything naturally.

Just when it seems that Zari's ability to hold her tongue and endure will last indefinitely, she finally finds her voice at her time of greatest pain: "The snake that had remained coiled up around her heart raised its head and struck."

Savushun is important, not only as a work of literature and a landmark in feminism, but also for the insights it provides for non-Iranians into the culture and habits of mind of a nation that, since the 1978–79 Islamic Revolution, has too often been lazily vilified in the West: Iran is not exclusively inhabited by religious fanatics any more than the United States is "the Great Satan." Daneshvar also provides a timely reminder of the attractions of Shiraz, beautifully situated in the Zagros Mountains.

NIGERIA

HALF OF A YELLOW SUN (2006)

CHIMAMANDA NGOZI ADICHIE

Set before and during the Nigerian Civil War (1967–70), *Half of a Yellow Sun*, by the Nigerian writer Chimamanda Ngozi Adichie (b. 1977), provides a powerful and compassionate insight into the impact of war on the lives of people swept up in it. It is essential reading for anyone visiting the country, or wanting to gain an insight into modern Nigeria, because many of the ethnic tensions that led to the war still remain today.

Nigeria achieved independence from Britain in 1960. Although numerous ethnic groups were widely distributed throughout the country, each of the three main peoples had its own geographical base: the Igbo in the east, the Hausa–Fulani in the north, and the Yoruba in the west.

This epic novel opens in the early 1960s, a period that looked at the time like the golden dawn of an emergent nation. Odenigbo, a math teacher at the newly established University of Nsukka, hires Ugwu, a rural peasant, as his houseboy, but he doesn't treat him as a menial— he encourages his learning and enrolls him in the local school. Odenigbo's girlfriend, later his wife, Olanna, is a daughter of a Lagos businessman and has a twin sister, Kainene. They are all Igbos (as is the author). The fifth main character is Kainene's lover, Richard Churchill, a white Englishman who has given up a job as a journalist in London to study—and, he hopes, write about—tribal art.

At the start of the book, the differences between the Igbos and the other indigenous peoples amount to little more than a comedy of manners; there seems no reason to foresee trouble. There is in general a pragmatic harmony between the groups: Olanna used to have a Hausa boyfriend; Odenigbo has a Yoruba colleague.

In Nigeria at this time, however, interethnic relations were gradually deteriorating. In September 1966 the massacre of perhaps as many as 30,000 Igbo in the Hausa area made around a million Igbos flee back to their ancestral districts, where they set about expelling other ethnicities from the lands they regarded as exclusively their own.

In May 1967, Igbo military leader General Ojukwu declared the eastern region of Nigeria the independent state of Biafra. (The flag of the breakaway nation bore the top half of a rising sun, and it is from this emblem that the book takes its title.) General Gowon, head of the federal

POSTCOLONIAL REVISIONISM

Odenigbo believes that part of the tainted legacy of colonialism is its "lines in the sand"—the creation of countries that were not countries before the white man came to colonize. He regards himself as an African and an Igbo, but not as a Nigerian, because there was no such place as Nigeria before the British invented it.

government, refused to recognize this secession and vowed to bring the rebels to heel. Before Biafra was eventually reincorporated into the Nigerian state in January 1970, possibly up to three million people died in battle or from starvation and disease; there were numerous atrocities.

Adichie shows the changes in her characters' fortunes and morale as they are caught up in the war. Many of them are diminished, particularly Odenigbo—previously a radical idealist, later reduced to drunken adultery—and Ugwo, who is conscripted into the Biafran military. Yet in this extreme adversity we see the great strength and resilience of Olanna, who adopts the child of Odenigbo's mistress and nurtures her even as her own circumstances deteriorate.

ABOVE *A symbol of reconciliation, this statue in Lagos represents the country's three main ethnicities supporting Nigeria together.*

A GRAIN OF WHEAT (1967)

NGŨGĨ WA THIONG'O

In this novel by the Kenyan writer Ngũgĩ wa Thiong'o (b. 1938), the terrain is memorably described. In the Rift Valley "the walls of the escarpment […] climbed in steps to the highlands; a row of smaller hills, some hewn round at the top while others bore scoops and volcano mouths, receded into shrouds of mist and mystery." The 19th-century colonization period is depicted in an array of colors: white men arrive with black books (Bibles); they are soon followed by red men with swords and "bamboo poles that vomited fire and smoke."

Against the topographical and historical background is set this powerful tale of Kenya on the eve of independence in 1963. When local hero Kihika is captured and hanged by the British, his fellow resistance fighters are certain that he would never have been caught if he hadn't been betrayed. Among the most prominent suspects is Karanja, who is known to have previously been an informant. Almost the only local African who's above suspicion is Mugo, a hero of the Uhuru

TITLE

Taken from the Bibles brought to Kenya by the first white settlers, the title of this novel refers to the Parable of the Grain of Wheat recounted in the Gospel of John in the Bible, in which Jesus teaches that, in order to get to Heaven, Christians must abandon the ego:

"Very truly I tell you, unless a kernel of wheat falls to the ground and dies, it remains only a single seed. But if it dies, it produces many seeds."

(John 12:24–26, New International Version, 1978)

("freedom") Movement who led a hunger strike while interned in a British concentration camp. Of course, all is not as it seems; everyone in the novel's fictional village of Thabai has mixed motives, and people are often best at hiding what they most need to conceal. And then there's the Swahili proverb *Kikulacho ki nguoni mwako* (literally, "that which eats you is within you"), which, roughly translated, means much the same as an oft-quoted line in *Modern Love*, George Meredith's 1891 sonnet sequence: "We are betrayed by what is false within."

LEFT *Remote countryside in Baringo County, part of the Rift Valley, around 170 miles (275km) northwest of Nairobi.*

DEMOCRATIC REPUBLIC OF THE CONGO
THE POISONWOOD BIBLE (1998)
BARBARA KINGSOLVER

In *The Poisonwood Bible* by the American writer Barbara Kingsolver (b. 1955), Nathan Price, a Baptist preacher, leaves his home in the US state of Georgia to work as a missionary in Kilanga, a small town in the Congo. With him he takes his wife and their four daughters.

Orleanna Price lacks her husband's evangelical zeal but has a pagan's appreciation for the Bible, being devoted to such phrases as "purge me with hyssop" (Psalm 51:7). The eldest child, Rachel, aged 15 at the start of the book, is a consumerist and a fashion victim. The twins, Leah and Adah, are 14 at the beginning. Leah is the devoted daughter, the one who takes her father's sayings as holy writ (which they mainly are). Adah has hemiplegia and is usually silent, although her verbal dexterity is prominent on the page—she is forever punning and finding palindromes. As she herself admits, "It is true I do not speak as well as I can think. But that is true of most people…' The youngest Price, Ruth May, is five years old at the outset.

The story is shared by Orleanna and her daughters as they each narrate their own dedicated chapters. Orleanna is the only one with hindsight; all the girls' accounts are apparently contemporaneous with the events they describe.

Conditions in their new surroundings are hostile in almost every way. There are mosquitoes, insects, spiders, snakes, and lions, all potentially life-threatening. The story opens in 1959, the year before the Belgian colony gained independence, amid instability and violence, at a time when white people became as unwelcome as they were already conspicuous.

Despite the deteriorating political situation, Nathan Price is not put off his messianic mission. His determination to carry out what he regards as God's will recalls Captain Ahab's obsessive pursuit of the whale in Herman Melville's *Moby-Dick* (1851). He disregards the villagers' traditional beliefs and their entirely rational fear of crocodiles in order to baptize their children in the Kwilu River.

Nathan interlards his sermons with words from the local language—though when he tries to tell them that Jesus is "precious and dear," he pronounces the word wrongly, saying that the Christian Son of God is the poisonwood tree (*Metopium toxiferum*), contact with which causes skin rashes. (Indeed, it injured Nathan himself when he ignored a warning about it soon after arriving in Africa.) Nathan is also oblivious to his own family's illnesses, and his obduracy has dire consequences for all of them.

Today, parts of the Democratic Republic of Congo are still unsafe; visitors are warned to keep away from the northern and eastern borders. However, Kilanga is not inaccessible. Located in Boko district, Pool region, it is about 125 miles (200km) southwest of the capital, Kinshasa (known as Léopoldville till 1966 and in the book). Wildlife tour packages are available.

THE NO. 1 LADIES' DETECTIVE AGENCY (1998)

ALEXANDER MCCALL SMITH

Many cities have a fictional detective, and in some of them—London, Paris, and New York are among those that spring to mind—it may almost seem as if there's a sleuth for every felon. Gaborone was not of their number until Alexander McCall Smith (b. 1948) made the capital of Botswana a crime scene in this novel, the first of a series of the same title, which at the start of 2019 comprised 19 books.

The setting is unique, and that's a big part of the charm. The streets aren't particularly mean, most of the crooks are small-time, and most of their crimes are silly rather than evil. The investigation bureau of the title is set up by Mma Precious Ramotswe (Mma is a term of respect for a woman), who finances the venture by selling her late father's cattle. She wonders at first whether there will be any demand for her services—after all, Gaborone has never had a private eye before—but supply creates demand, and gradually a trickle of clients emerges.

The first case gives a reliable taste of things to come. A woman asks Mma Ramotswe to find out whether the man who's recently moved in with her is really, as he claims to be, the father she's never previously met. Suspecting at once that he's a con man, Mma Ramotswe tells him that his daughter has been seriously injured and needs a transfusion of blood of a type so rare that only a close relative will have it… The suspect suddenly recalls that he is not her father after all, and he is soon run out of town.

In a later case, Mma Ramotswe unmasks an insurance scammer who has claimed at different times to have lost the same finger through the negligence of three different employers. Forensic science and clinical analysis are not for Mma Precious Ramotswe; she works mainly on instinct and feminine intuition.

McCall Smith's descriptions of Gaborone and the surrounding countryside—a land with no end to it, where "a man could walk, or ride, forever, and he would never get anywhere"—draw deeply on his knowledge of the terrain: he's a Scot who spent his childhood in Bulawayo, Southern Rhodesia (modern Zimbabwe), and later taught law at the University of Botswana.

HEART OF LIGHTNESS

Botswana is an oasis of calm in the midst of an often turbulent continent. As Mma Ramotswe's father, Obed, remarks, "There's no other country in Africa that can hold its head up as we can. We have no political prisoners, and never have had any. We have democracy. We have been careful. The Bank of Botswana is full of money, from our diamonds."

ABOVE *Built in 1966 and now fully modernized, the President Hotel, where Mma Ramotswe likes to take tea on the veranda, is part of the US Cresta hotel group.*

GABORONE TOURS

Many of the real-life locations in the series feature in guided tours of Gaborone. Among the highlights are the private house (not open to the public) that inspired Mma Ramotswe's house and office in the books; the Botswana Book Centre, her favorite store; and the President Hotel, where she enjoyed sipping tea on the veranda. About 25 miles (41km) northeast of the capital is another literary pilgrimage site: Mochudi, where Precious grew up. The road between these two places crosses the railway line at Pilane, where her mother was hit by a train.

ZIMBABWE
THE GRASS IS SINGING (1950)
DORIS LESSING

The African setting is unnamed, but since we are told that it is not the Republic of South Africa and that it is a British possession within walking distance of Nyasaland (modern Malawi), there is no doubt that the country described here in rich detail is what was at the time of publication Southern Rhodesia (now Zimbabwe). It is where Doris Lessing (1919–2013) grew up.

The Grass is Singing (the title is a quotation from T. S. Eliot's poem *The Waste Land*) opens with a newspaper report about the murder of a white woman, Mary Turner, by her black servant, a Bantu named Moses. We soon learn that there is more to this affair than the brief printed snippet suggests, and we may at first anticipate a whodunit. But Lessing's purpose here is quite different: Moses really has killed his boss, and the rest of the book is an account of how the tragedy unfolded.

It begins when Mary, until now reasonably content with her life in an urban center—again unnamed, but probably Salisbury (now Harare), or possibly Bulawayo—is thrown into emotional turmoil after overhearing people wondering why she's past 30 and still single. Partly in reaction to this malicious gossip, she marries Dick, a quixotic 55-year-old farmer known to some of his acquaintance as "Jonah" because every moneymaking scheme he tries on his farm ends in expensive failure. (And he refuses to cultivate the one crop almost guaranteed to make him money—tobacco—because the method of growing it strikes him as too mechanistic and industrial.)

Mary tries to adapt to life in the remote countryside, but poverty and heat grind her down. Her neuroses surface in various ways: sometimes as rows with her husband, and at other times as excessive strictness toward her African employees, whom she regards as savages. On one occasion she lashes out with a whip, an action that shocks her almost as much as her victim.

Lessing describes the Rhodesian/Zimbabwean terrain at all times of the year. A typically vivid passage describes Mary first setting eyes on her new marital home in the countryside:

LEFT *Under white rule until 1980, Harare, Zimbabwe, was formerly known as Salisbury, Southern Rhodesia. Doris Lessing lived in Salisbury for 12 years as a young woman, and when she left for London in 1949, she had the manuscript for* The Grass Is Singing *in her suitcase.*

ABOVE *Oxen plowing the red earth of a rural Zimbabwean farm.*

"The moon had gone behind a great luminous white cloud, and it was suddenly very dark—miles of darkness under a dimly starlit sky. All around were trees, the squat, flattened trees of the high veld, which seem as if pressure of sun has distorted them, looking now like vague dark presences standing about the small clearing…"

JUSTIFYING INJUSTICE

A lifelong left-winger, Doris Lessing observed that, while most of the world's people in the late 1940s were influenced by perceptions of class, whites in southern Africa thought principally in terms of race. She wrote that European newcomers to Southern Rhodesia who expressed misgivings about colonial treatment of the natives would be told that they needed to "become used to the country." This defensive response found an echo in the 1970s and '80s, when a standard apologist's response to criticism of the Apartheid regime began with "How much time have you spent in South Africa?"

A DRY WHITE SEASON (1979)

ANDRÉ BRINK

Apartheid ended in South Africa in 1994, but that does nothing to diminish the power of this novel by Afrikaner novelist André Brink (1935–2015) about the evils of white minority rule.

We gather at the outset that the ending will be tragic. Far from being a spoiler, that knowledge heightens the sense of the malevolent power of the state, the depressing certainty that resistance is useless.

Ben Du Toit is a white teacher who helps Gordon Ngubene, a black janitor at his Johannesburg school, to find out what happened to Gordon's son, Jonathan, who disappeared after being picked up by the Security Police during a demonstration in the black township of Soweto in 1976. At first, the authorities deny all knowledge of Jonathan; then, when Gordon and Ben show them the statements of witnesses who saw him in jail and in hospital, they say he died of a heart attack and they hadn't known whom to contact.

There is plenty to suggest that Jonathan was murdered, but evidence goes missing and witnesses are intimidated. When Gordon shows no sign of being put off the pursuit of justice, he, too, is picked up by the police and is later said to have hanged himself in his cell after admitting being a terrorist.

Ben is a liberal who has hitherto believed that the authorities will always be doing their best, but these events undermine his faith in South African justice. His attempts to challenge the system are thwarted at almost every turn.

The police begin by appealing to what they regard as his interests—why should he waste his time trying to find out what happened to black men? Next comes the suggestion that any white man who attempts to improve the lot of the African either is a Soviet agent or has been unwittingly subverted by communism; the red menace is everywhere.

When these approaches fail to put Ben off the scent, the threats become more physical. His house is searched, his tires are slashed, his phone is tapped, he gets sent a bomb in the mail, warning shots are fired...

Ben becomes known as a man who helps blacks, so many of them come to him for assistance, which he cannot provide. Meanwhile, his white friends desert him, his headmaster disapproves, and his marriage disintegrates.

As the end approaches, Captain Stolz of the Security Police makes one final man-to-man appeal to Ben. When that, too, fails to have the desired effect, Ben is knocked down and killed by a car. The driver is never identified, and the official version of events is that Ben was on his way to post a letter— but since no letter was found on his body, how could that be true? Under white minority rule, it doesn't matter that the lie is incredible: the police, the coroners, the doctors, and the courts are all so corrupt that refutation is unachievable.

A Dry White Season was at first banned in South Africa, but was published by the author via an underground press. A 1989 film adaptation was also banned initially.

RIGHT *Modern Soweto. The Soweto uprising of 1976 is the background to the events depicted in this novel.*

A TOWN LIKE ALICE

THE WHITE TIGER

AN ARTIST OF THE FLOATING WORLD

THE GOOD EARTH

CHAPTER 4

ASIA AND AUSTRALASIA

AZERBAIJAN

ALI AND NINO (1937)

KURBAN SAID

Ali and Nino is now sometimes described as the official novel of Azerbaijan (even though the original text was in German), and readers may find it easy to see why: the work seems to counsel tolerance and coexistence in a region of the world where such attitudes have not always been common.

BOOMING BAKU

Modern Azerbaijan is a secular state. Although more than 90 percent of the population is Muslim, do not expect to see all the women in the hijab—Islamic dress codes are more commonly observed in London than on the streets of Baku, the capital and the largest city on the Caspian Sea. Nor will visitors find that companies pull down their shutters at sunset on Friday: the business of Azerbaijan is business. The main source of the nation's modern prosperity is oil, which is abundant throughout the region and particularly beneath the Caspian Sea. The good to which the post-communist government has put its wealth is miraculous to behold—modern visitors to Baku will have to delve back into the history books to remind themselves that, between the collapse of the short-lived Democratic Republic in 1920 and the end of communism in 1991, this city was the capital of a Soviet Socialist Republic. Comparisons are odious, but Baku is much more Paris than Minsk.

The scion of an aristocratic Muslim family, Ali is first exposed to other religious ideas at his school in Russia in the years immediately preceding the 1917 Bolshevik Revolution. He falls in love with Nino, a Christian princess from Georgia. At first Nino is reluctant to reciprocate Ali's affection, since she fears being forced to take the veil or join a harem, but he promises that such things will never happen to her.

Nino is then kidnapped by Melik Nachararyan, an Armenian Christian. Ali pursues them, stabs him to death, and rescues her. The reunited couple take to the Caucasus Mountains of Dagestan to avoid the vengeance of Melik's family. They marry in a small town near Makhachkala and live a rural idyll, poor but happy, until the revolution changes everything.

Ali and Nino take miserable refuge in Tehran, Iran, but then the establishment in 1918 of the Azerbaijan Democratic Republic attracts them to Baku. It is there, in the walled Old City within the city, that the remainder of the novel is set, during the two years leading up to the Bolsheviks' victory in 1920, when the country was incorporated into the Soviet Union.

BELOW *Ancient and modern in happy coexistence: the Old City of Baku with, in the background, the 1,017-ft (310-m) TV Tower (with revolving restaurant) and the 600-ft (183-m) Flame Towers. Part of* Ali and Nino *is set in the Old City during the short-lived Azerbaijan republic.*

AFGHANISTAN
THE KITE RUNNER (2003)
KHALED HOSSEINI

ABOVE *Rural life in Afghanistan before the 1979 Soviet invasion.*

When this novel opens, in the early 1970s, Afghanistan is a contented backwater and a holiday destination for Western hippies attracted by natives who "cherish custom but abhor rules." In Kabul, the young narrator, Amir, has a privileged upbringing that is generally happy but not idyllic. His relationship with Baba, his father, is complicated by the fact that his mother died giving birth to him.

Amir has his own servant boy, Hassan, a year younger than himself, who helps him at kite-flying competitions. On one occasion, Hassan saves Amir from a gang of local bullies, but on a subsequent occasion, when the tables are turned, Amir leaves Hassan to be gruesomely brutalized by the same thugs.

In 1979 Afghanistan is invaded by the Soviet Union. Amir flees with his father to the USA and there makes a happy marriage and a name for himself as a writer. But he does not escape his sense of guilt about betraying his childhood friend, who is left behind.

Meanwhile Amir's native land becomes a suburb of Hell: the Russians withdraw and the country is overrun by the Taliban, extremist religious fanatics. Back in California, Baba grows old and ill. When news of his death reaches Afghanistan, long-broken contacts are renewed. Amir returns to Kabul in the hope of helping Hassan and his family. There he witnesses horrors: a man on the street trying to sell his own artificial leg in order to raise enough money to feed his children; a halftime entertainment at a football match that involves the stoning to death of an adulterous couple; a children's home whose director has to prostitute some of those in his care in order to protect the majority. Then Amir comes face to face once more with the leader of the bullies, who has risen to eminence in the Taliban and has lost none of the sadism he displayed in his youth.

Although Amir's deliverance from evil may briefly stretch credibility, this is a small blemish in an otherwise remarkably assured and powerful debut novel by Khaled Hosseini (b. 1965). Though himself an Afghan émigré to the USA, he has created a fully imagined world and—perhaps most laudably—an ending that is tentatively optimistic rather than simplistically happy. No doubt many more years will pass before Afghanistan is again a realistic destination for anyone other than military personnel and aid workers, but *The Kite Runner* can only whet the traveler's appetite to explore the country at the earliest opportunity.

INDIA

SHANTARAM (2003)

GREGORY DAVID ROBERTS

The Australian author of *Shantaram*, Gregory David Roberts (b. 1952), was convicted of armed robbery in 1978, then two years later escaped from prison in Australia and fled to Bombay (Mumbai), where he avoided recapture for a decade and lived the life described in this long and compelling book.

At least, that's one version of the background. However, plenty of the people supposedly depicted have popped up to deny any resemblance between themselves and the text. And whenever the "autobiographical" label gets too tightly attached to the work, Roberts protests in interviews that most of the events set in India and all of the characters are invented.

This uncertainty about where the facts end and the fiction begins does not diminish the attraction of *Shantaram*; on the contrary, it may enhance the book's appeal. Readers can try to sift truth from invention—or at least what they regard as credible from incredible—as they go along. They may struggle with some of the dialogue, the sententiousness ("Truth is a bully we all pretend to like"), the specious definitions ("Magic, the trick that connects the ordinary to the impossible"), and some of the author's assumptions about what needs to be explained ("India is about six times the size of France... but it has almost twenty times the population"). However, the plot is so rich and varied that these are no more than tiny smudges on an immense canvas that fills the horizon and features an abundance of sex, love, drugs, disease, robbery, prison, Bollywood, smuggling, philanthropy, and exploitation.

The title, a Maharashtrian word meaning "man of God's peace," is the name given to the narrator by the mother of his Indian friend Prabhaker, who had originally called him Lin, meaning "penis."

Shantaram has a huge cast of characters, many of them larger than life but none of them overshadowing the setting: Bombay itself, in all its teeming glory. The sights, the smells, the tastes, the wealth of the downtown, and the poverty of the Navy Nagar seaside slum at the southern tip are all vividly described in ways that will evoke the city for those who know it and inspire those who don't to see it for themselves.

RIGHT *As part of a traditional annual ritual, an image of the Hindu goddess Durga is about to be immersed in the sea in Mumbai.*

INDIA

THE WHITE TIGER (2008)

ARAVIND ADIGA

Set mainly in Delhi and Bangalore, this debut novel by a former financial journalist captures the vibrancy and some of the beauty of those cities without airbrushing out the chaos and poverty that also characterize them. Aravind Adiga (b. 1974) presents a panorama that, though warts-and-all, should encourage prospective travelers to experience for themselves the paradoxes of a rich nation that still has too many paupers, an emerging global power that is simultaneously new-tech and neolithic.

India is, of course, too diverse to encapsulate in a single work of fiction. It has more faces than it has gods, who, according to Balram Halwai, the hero of this book, number 36 million if you count all the Hindu deities, or 36 million and four if you add the God of Islam and the Christian Trinity of God the Father, God the Son, and God the Holy Spirit.

Balram wonders briefly which of these divinities he should worship and quickly decides none of them. He is out for himself, determined to escape what everyone around him in his rural village regards as his inevitable fate—to become either a rickshaw-puller, like his father, or a sweet-maker, like members of his caste since time immemorial.

Balram takes his first step along a different path when he becomes the number two chauffeur to a rich family. Discovering that the number one driver, Ram Persad, is a secret Muslim, he loses no time in denouncing him to their Hindu employer and getting him fired. In bed at night

Balram briefly pauses to reflect on what a hard life the man has had, and how he is a much better driver than Balram himself. But the moment soon passes. Balram continues, "I turned to the other side, farted, and went back to sleep."

From there Balram's ascent is swift and bloody. He moves to Delhi, where he witnesses corruption at the highest levels of Indian society. Deciding that the only way to make further progress is by stealing, he slits his boss's throat and makes off with a bag full of cash intended as a bribe for a politician. In one of the classic novels that are said to have influenced Adiga, *Crime and Punishment* (1866) by Fyodor Dostoyevsky, the protagonist, Raskolnikov, having committed a murder, is wracked by guilt. No such introspection inhibits Balram, who moves to a new location, adopts an alias, and founds a

STYLISH TOUCH

How does Adiga announce his talent? Right from the outset, he takes a rhetorical device that can be annoying in literature—speech marks—and turns it to comic advantage by making the framework of the book a series of letters he writes, but doesn't send, to Wen Jiabao, the real-life premier of China at the time of publication, with whom the protagonist adopts a chatty and familiar tone throughout.

BELOW *Live chickens for sale at a market in Delhi near Jama Masjid, one of the largest mosques in India.*

taxi company: one of the many start-ups that are transforming the Indian economy.

One of the major themes of *The White Tiger* is the clash between the values of those who live in poverty—what Balram terms "the Darkness"—and those who live comfortably in "the Light" that only wealth can bring. The problem, as the hero sees it, is that most Indians are trapped in what he calls "the Rooster Coop": like the fowl confined in the old market of Delhi, they can see their fate—hundreds of the birds are slaughtered every day—and yet they make no effort to avert it. But Balram is no rooster; he sees himself as a white tiger destined to escape the cage. In the words of a poet whose name he can never remember: "I was looking for the key for years / But the door was always open."

Also subjected to sharp criticism here is the dishonesty that is portrayed as endemic and institutionalized. Balram's father voted in

PROPHET WITHOUT HONOR IN HIS OWN COUNTRY

The White Tiger won the 2008 Booker Prize, awarded in England, but Adiga's depiction of his native land did not go down so well in India itself. There, many readers thought that the book perpetuated outmoded stereotypes, such as that reflected in an incident in which Balram's boss and his boss's wife—Ashok and Pinky Madam—argue about the correct pronunciation of the word "pizza."

12 elections but never set foot inside a voting booth; in return for regular payments, the police make hit-and-run fatalities disappear from their accident reports.

CHINA
THE GOOD EARTH (1931)
PEARL S. BUCK

The Good Earth by American author Pearl S. Buck (1892–1973) gave the West an unprecedented insight into China before the 1949 communist revolution. In spite of the rapid development of the nation's economy since then, the depiction of Chinese rural life and land in the book and the 1937 film version retains much of its authenticity even today.

The novel describes the lives of peasant farmer Wang Lung and his industrious wife, O-Lan, who works with him in the fields before and after giving birth to their first child. They earn enough money from the sale of their excess harvest to buy some land from the House of Hwang, which has fallen into debt through profligacy.

On their expanded landholding the couple continue to prosper, and O-Lan gives birth to another son and a daughter. But then sorrows come, not single spies but in battalions. Wang Lung overstretches by spending the family savings

on additional land just before a harvest fails. The region is hit by famine, and O-Lan strangles her fourth child at birth because there is nothing to feed her on.

Starving and destitute, Wang Lung sells his furniture to raise enough money to take his family on a firewagon (steam train) to a city in the south. Here they live in a hut and Wang Lung pulls a rickshaw while his wife and children beg on the street.

Wang Lung observes the immense gulf between his own poverty and the wealth of Chinese aristocrats and foreigners. Revolution is in the air, and when the rich are driven out, Wang Lung and his wife are among the peasants who loot the abandoned mansions. Now laden with stolen gold and jewelry, they return to the north, go back to work in their fields, and prosper again. They buy additional land from the now bankrupt House of Hwang; they hire laborers to work on their farm; O-Lan has more children (twins).

But Wang Lung tires of his wife and takes a mistress, Lotus, a manipulative courtesan. He is besotted with her for a while and disregards both his wife's distress and his father's disapproval, until Lotus is cruel to one of his children. At that point, he finally sees her in her true light, pulls himself together, and gets back to work.

His eldest son is lazy and a womanizer; Wang Lung has to arrange a marriage for him to keep him out of trouble. Wang Lung's uncle, a gangster, demands a share of his wealth, but Wang Lung tames him by getting him addicted to opium. O-Lan and Wang Lung's father die in quick

CELEBRATED AUTHOR

Born in the United States and brought up in Zhenjiang, where her parents were Presbyterian missionaries, Pearl S. Buck won a Pulitzer Prize for this novel in 1932. She followed it with *Sons* (1932) and *A House Divided* (1935). The three works were then published as a trilogy, *The House of Earth* (also 1935). In 1938 she was awarded the Nobel Prize in Literature, for her "rich and truly epic descriptions of peasant life in China and for her biographical masterpieces."

succession, but his children start to have children of their own.

Eventually Wang Lung acquires the whole of the Hwang estate. He has servants and farm workers, and he heads a dynasty of three generations. But neither his worldly success nor his new concubine, Pear Blossom, can satisfy him; the only certainty, in his worldview, is the ownership of land. It's the importance of land that he stresses most strongly to his two eldest sons as he approaches death—but at the end of the book there is a strong suggestion that they plan to sell it as soon as he dies.

THE BLUE SKY (1994)

GALSAN TSCHINAG

The traditional way of life of the Tuvan nomads of Mongolia is under threat from the largely malign external forces of progress, pollution, and politics. But within the *ail* (family settlement) featured in this autobiographical novel by the Mongolian writer Galsan Tschinag (b. 1944), the old customs are maintained against the odds. The herders move their yurts from place to place according to the seasons along the upper course of Ak-Hem, "the milky-white mother river," a tributary of the Yenisei.

THE AUTHOR

Galsan Tschinag is the adopted name of Irgit Shynykbai-oglu Dshurukuwaa, a Tuvan born in Mongolia in 1944. He is a poet and a shaman as well as a novelist. Tschinag went to university in Leipzig and now writes in German. Between his graduation in 1976 and the fall of communism in 1990, he was regarded with suspicion by the rulers of the Soviet Union, of which Mongolia was then a part—but since Mongolia became independent, his work has been published throughout the world. *The Blue Sky* was the first part of a projected trilogy; the second volume, *The Gray Earth*, was published in German in 1999 and in English in 2010. The final volume is *The White Mountain*, published in German in 2000 and in English in 2019.

The narrator, whom we first encounter as a child, is not neglected by his parents, but they are busy working, so his strongest youthful attachments are to his grandmother and to his dog, Arsylang.

The novel—reputedly the first written imaginative account of a culture that has previously been maintained exclusively by oral tradition—is full of insights into life in the Altai Mountains. For example, in English, the expression "to send word" is largely figurative, almost always referring to some form of written communication. In the Tuvans' Turkic language, however, the equivalent term means exactly that: riders leaving one *ail* are told messages to repeat verbatim at the settlement for which they're bound. The Tuvan equivalent of the Tooth Fairy is another of the many things that make this book worth reading, even by those who have no intention of visiting Mongolia.

BELOW *Herders driving yak across a plain in the Altai Mountains west of Ölgii.*

AN ARTIST OF THE FLOATING WORLD (1986)

KAZUO ISHIGURO

This novel by Japanese-born British Nobel laureate Kazuo Ishiguro (b. 1954) is set in Japan following World War 2. The fictional protagonist, Masuji Ono, is now an old man, looking back on his life. In his prime he was the outstanding member of a radical school of artists who painted courtesans, geishas, and low-life bars. But he later became convinced that Japan needed to be self-assertive abroad, and so his paintings in the 1930s and early '40s were propaganda for imperialism and the war effort.

Ono's work remained popular until 1945, when Japan was defeated and occupied by US forces. Many of the nation's generals and top businessmen were executed, or were sacked from their jobs, or committed suicide to atone for leading the nation to disaster; even a composer of patriotic songs killed himself. Ono and his work fell into disfavor, and when the novel opens, in 1948, the future is American: Ono's young grandson has never heard of samurai warriors but has had his imagination captured by the Lone Ranger.

The character of Masuji Ono is sometimes described as an example of the "unreliable narrator," and his account of his life is indeed self-regarding and self-exculpatory. However, it represents events and other people accurately enough for readers to see what he himself fails to recognize: that he has plenty to be ashamed of, and his past is coming back to haunt him. A family whose son is contemplating marriage to the artist's daughter carries out a background check (a normal procedure, we learn, in traditional Japan). It reveals that during the war Ono had informed on his favorite pupil, who had consequently been tortured by the secret police.

At the *miai* (the party at which the families of the prospective bride and groom are formally introduced to each other) Ono is given an opportunity to acknowledge his misdeeds. Eventually he admits, "All I can say is that at the time I acted in good faith. I believed in all sincerity I was achieving good for my fellow countrymen. But as you see, I am not now afraid to admit I was mistaken."

To this, his interlocutor, the groom's father, reassuringly responds, "I'm sure you're too harsh on yourself, Mr Ono." Thereafter the artist's life goes back to normal, and at the end of the book he is every bit as complacent as he was at the outset.

The many places named here are Ishiguro's inventions but they are all in their own way authentically Japanese. This novel captures the look and atmosphere of the nation as well as one of its major modern preoccupations—war guilt.

RIGHT *A geisha walking in the rain along Pontocho, a Kyoto alley renowned for its bars, restaurants, and exclusive clubs.*

NORWEGIAN WOOD (1987)

HARUKI MURAKAMI

In life, many things may trigger involuntary memory. In literature, one of the most famous instances of the phenomenon occurs when the narrator dunks a madeleine in his tea at the beginning of Proust's 1913 novel *À la recherche du temps perdu* (*In Search of Lost Time*).

Another well-attested mnemonic stimulus is music, especially pop—as the heroine of Noël Coward's 1930 play *Private Lives* remarks, "Extraordinary how potent cheap music is." And so it proves for Toru Watanabe, protagonist of the celebrated novel by Japanese writer Haruki Murakami (b. 1949). *Norwegian Wood* takes its title from a track on The Beatles' 1965 album *Rubber Soul*. On hearing "a sweet orchestral cover version" of the love song piped through the overhead speakers of the plane that has just landed him in Hamburg, Watanabe's mind is immediately transported back nearly 20 years to his late teens in Tokyo. It was then that the suicide of his best friend Kizuki drew him into an ill-fated relationship with the dead boy's former girlfriend, Naoko.

A STROLL DOWN MEMORY LANE

Tokyo is described in *Norwegian Wood* with such precision that readers can retrace some of Watanabe's footsteps. When he meets Naoko again after many years apart, he follows her on a roughly arc-shaped walk through central Tokyo. To take the same route, start at Yotsuya railway station, and turn right at Iidabashi, coming out at the moat. Cross the intersection at Jinbocho, and climb the hill at Ochanomizu as far as Hongo. Now follow the tram tracks to Komagome. Total distance: just over 6 miles (10km).

Norwegian Wood is a coming-of-age novel—but, unlike many works of its kind, it does not bear out Benjamin Disraeli's contention (in his 1837 novel *Henrietta Temple*), "The magic of first love is our ignorance that it can ever end." In *Norwegian Wood*, all the characters and subsequent events subsist in the shadow of Kizuki's fate, and his is not the only self-inflicted death described here.

As Watanabe's recollections come flooding back, his abiding concern that he might have forgotten important details impels him to re-invoke the Japanese capital in minute and painful detail.

LEFT *Every spring throughout Japan, used books are sold on open-air stalls in a festival that aims to encourage reading.*

THAILAND

THE BEACH (1996)

ALEX GARLAND

Thailand's tourist trade began as a trickle in the 1960s and quickly turned into a torrent. In many of the years since then, Bangkok has welcomed more foreign visitors than any other city in the world apart from London.

Provincial Thailand quickly developed to meet increasing demand. The most easily accessible of the hundreds of islands along the coast soon became resorts with all mod cons, aspiring to attract Western vacationers who were looking for something more exotic than southern Spain. But one of the joys of Thailand is that there are other islands that have yet to be commercialized, and it was to such undiscovered gems that Western budget travelers beat a path in the 1980s and '90s.

One such adventurer is Richard, the hero of this novel by Alex Garland (b. 1970). Accompanied by a young French couple, he strikes out from Bangkok's Khao San Road, "a decompression chamber for those about to leave or enter Thailand, a halfway house between East and West"—and goes in search of a secret beach on a hard-to-reach island off Koh Samui. Once there they discover that it's only a semi-idyll, as it is divided into two zones: an area for sybarites and a cannabis farm guarded by armed criminals. When the two communities rub up against each other, it falls to Richard to patrol the frontier of his territory. This task enables him to play out real-life versions of his beloved Atari and Nintendo video games and indulge his fantasies about the Vietnam War, a conflict that he knows about only through movies such as *Apocalypse Now* (1979) and *Platoon* (1986).

ISLANDS IN THE SUN

The most popular Thai island is Phuket. Next is Koh Samui (Koh or Ko means "island"), and not far behind it in visitor numbers is neighboring Koh Pha Ngan. Also recommended by Condé Nast Traveller are Koh Tao, Koh Lanta, Koh Lipe, Koh Chang, Koh Phi Phi, the Similan Islands, and Koh Si Chang.

AUTHOR AS CARTOGRAPHER

The novel was adapted into a film of the same name in 2000. Directed by Danny Boyle and starring Leonardo DiCaprio, it was shot on Koh Phi Phi Ley (near Koh Phi Phi). The map that appears in the film was illustrated by Alex Garland, author of the book.

The Beach is a highly readable adventure story with suspense, jeopardy, pursuit, escape, blood and gore, and drugs. The only item missing from the expected features of a blockbuster is sex, which is conspicuous by its absence from all but the opening scene in Bangkok.

VIETNAM

THE SORROW OF WAR (1990)

BAO NINH

What's in a name? "Bao Ninh" is the pseudonym of Hoang Ấu Phương (b. 1952); it is the name of the village in which his father grew up. His book was originally called *Nỗi buồn chiến tranh* (*The Destiny of Love*), but the publisher of the English language edition insisted that the title be changed to *The Sorrow of War*. This alteration leaves no doubt about the subject matter: the conflict that in the West is known as the Vietnam War and in Vietnam itself as Khổng chiến chống Mỹ (The War Against America). The English translation of the novel gave the Anglophone world a rare opportunity to see the conflict from a non-American perspective; readers in the West were then struck by the similarities in attitudes and behavior on both sides of the Demilitarized Zone.

Kien, the main character—a writer and victim of post-traumatic stress disorder—is very like his creator, who joined the North Vietnamese Army in 1969 at the age of 17. The author was one of only 10 members of his 500-strong unit to survive the war, which ended in 1975.

In a powerful reflection of Kien's tormented mind, the narrative flits back and forth between the postwar present and some of the most harrowing episodes of the conflict. It opens in the immediate aftermath of the war, when Kien is helping to clear corpses from the Jungle of Screaming Souls, an eerie place in which "ghosts and devils were born… [and are] still loose, wandering in every corner and bush… drifting along the stream, refusing to depart for the Other World."

There are flashbacks to the days when bullets were known as "bronze candy" and "country girls would give themselves to the boys… in return for a bra." It is such memories that give this book much of its power—these and the descriptions, particularly of a US bombing raid on Thanh Hóa and a cross-country journey to the Cambodian frontier.

CROCODILE LAKE

One of the most important locations in *The Sorrow of War*, Crocodile Lake (Bau Sau) is now a visitor attraction in Cát Tiên National Park, a vast lowland rainforest on the Đồng Nai River, 190 miles (306km) north of Saigon/Ho Chi Minh City and around the same distance south of Dalat. The reptiles that give this expanse of water its name were once plentiful here but were eradicated during the war by Agent Orange and other defoliants; more recently they have been reintroduced, and there are now around 200 of them in residence. There are also gibbons, elephants, leopards, snakes, possibly tigers, and more than 300 species of birds, some of which, such as the Siamese fireback (*Lophura diardi*), are extremely rare. But don't expect to encounter many of these creatures: most of them are shy, and they have 280 square miles (720sq km) of territory in which to stay out of sight.

ABOVE *Bau Sau is now restored to its former glory as a beauty spot and a haven for a rich variety of wildlife.*

A TOWN LIKE ALICE (1950)

NEVIL SHUTE

In London in the early 1950s, Jean Paget, a shorthand secretary at a ladies' shoe and handbag manufacturer, inherits a sum of money so large that she need never work again. She has no immediate plans, so she takes her time considering her options with the help of Noel Strachan, the book's narrator and the solicitor administering the estate of which she is the sole beneficiary.

Having spent World War 2 in Malaya, where she suffered under the Japanese occupation of that country, Jean first decides to return there to build a well in the village where she last lived before being repatriated at the end of the conflict. There she discovers that Joe Harman, a soldier who helped her during the war, has not died, as she thought, but has made it back home to Australia.

BELOW *Alice Springs today, more than half a century after it inspired both Neville Shute and his female protagonist.*

So Jean next heads Down Under to look him up. She goes first to Alice Springs, where she is greatly impressed by the quality of life. She then heads to Willstown, a fictional town in the Outback, where Joe runs a cattle station, or at least he does normally—when she gets there she learns that he, having also come into some money (in his case a lottery win), has gone to England to look for her.

In London Joe gets drunk and into trouble. Noel Strachan bails him out and advises him to sail back to Australia, but he doesn't tell Joe exactly why he thinks this is a good idea.

When Jean and Joe are finally reunited, they try to turn Willstown into "a town like Alice." First Jean sets up a workshop for making shoes out of crocodile skin. When this business starts to prosper, she opens ancillary shops, including an ice-cream parlor and—an important amenity for such a hot climate—a public swimming pool.

Immensely popular when first published, *A Town Like Alice* by Nevil Shute (1899–1960) has since rather fallen out of fashion. But there's plenty to admire here, including fluent prose and the picture of rough, inhospitable terrain being turned into a comfortable environment by immigrants. Also laudable, especially in view of the fact that this is essentially a romance, is the acknowledgment of some of the problems within this emergent society, not least the treatment of Aboriginal Australians.

At the start of the novel Jean Paget's present is London; her past is Malaya; and her future, it turns out, is Australia. The only way she can get to the future is via her past. *A Town Like Alice* is a novel of self-discovery and introspection, but not the introspection of the intellectual—it's established at the start that Jean has no knowledge of or interest in the life of the mind, and no desire to alter that state of affairs. She's a doer, not a thinker.

FLIGHT TO AUSTRALIA

Nevil Shute Norway—he dropped the Norway from his literary persona—was born in London in 1899 and became an aeronautical engineer. After serving in both World Wars, he flew his own plane to and from Australia in the company of another author, James Riddell, who wrote an account of their adventure, *Flight of Fancy* (1951). The journey confirmed Shute's suspicion that his native country of Britain was washed up, so shortly afterward he emigrated with his family to Australia. There he wrote both this novel and *On the Beach* (1957), a pessimistic vision of the post-Hiroshima age. Nevil Shute died in Melbourne in 1960.

OSCAR AND LUCINDA (1988)

PETER CAREY

It is most unusual for a work of art whose influences and antecedents are so readily apparent to be groundbreaking and original, but *Oscar and Lucinda* is a most unusual novel. It takes plot points and symbolism from old classics and spices them up in captivating new ways.

The young orphan, the coming-of-age/rite of passage, the quest for identity, the Oedipal conflict, the inheritance of considerable wealth, the human-versus-nature struggle, the doomed expedition into wilderness—these events have parallels in many works. Among them are Charlotte Brontë's *Jane Eyre* (1847), Emily Brontë's *Wuthering Heights* (1847), Herman Melville's *Moby-Dick* (1851), Charles Dickens's *Great Expectations* (1861), Joseph Conrad's *Heart of Darkness* (1899), and Edmund Gosse's *Father and Son* (1907). Also

present in Oscar and Lucinda are reminders of *Fitzcarraldo* (1982), Werner Herzog's movie about one man's attempt to haul a ship over a mountain in South America.

Peter Carey (b. 1943) has plenty of roots—and shows them—but he is not derivative. The magic additional ingredient is the force that brings the two title characters together and drives them forward: betting. Both Oscar and Lucinda are victims of this disease, though their forms of gambling have different symptoms—one is obsessional, the other compulsive.

They meet late in the novel on a boat from England to Australia. On the basis of the flip of a coin, Oscar has decided to emigrate to the southern hemisphere in order to convert the Aborigines to Christianity. Lucinda, heiress to a glassmaking factory in Darling Harbour, Sydney, is returning home after a year-long trip to the Old Country has failed to unearth the hoped-for husband.

On arrival, to Oscar, "Sydney was a blinding place. It made him squint." The Harbour "had a silver skin." Also striking is the weather: "August is the first month of the westerly—rude, bullying winds that cut across from Drummoyne or scream down from Bedlam Point and Hen and Chicken Bay."

LEFT *A historic 19th-century house in the Sydney suburb of Paddington.*

Through Oscar, the reader gradually gets to know the city's layout: first the downtown (George Street, St Andrew's Cathedral, the taverns in Paddington), and later the suburbs (Rushcutters Bay, Parramatta, White Bay, "… the edge of Balmain… down along that rocky promontory which ends in Longmore Point").

It is not long before the couple's late-night card-playing scandalizes the established Church and secular Sydneysiders alike. Outcasts from polite society, Oscar and Lucinda decide to gamble everything on building a glass church and transporting it to a new parish on the edge of the Outback in up-country New South Wales.

ABOVE *Where Oscar and Lucinda ended up: up the Bellinger River, a barrier estuary in central New South Wales.*

The latter part of the book takes us to Gleniffer and toward the source of the Bellinger River. Today there is a tourist park here, just off the Pacific Highway 260 miles (420km) north of Sydney, and around the same distance south of Brisbane.

THE LUMINARIES (2013)

ELEANOR CATTON

Near the beginning of this book of more than 800 pages, we read that someone asked a question, received a reply, then asked it once more. The interviewee didn't repeat his original answer but "bowed again and affirmed that this was precisely his meaning." The choice of words here is a sign that we can forget the year of publication—this is more than a 21st-century work set in the 1860s; it's a full-blown 19th-century novel.

Yet *The Luminaries*, by Canadian-born New Zealand author Eleanor Catton (b. 1985), is not a pastiche. Nor is it a Wilkie Collins retread (notwithstanding that one may imagine Catton ingesting *The Woman in White* (1860) with her mother's milk). It's a vibrantly original work of linguistic verve with a structure that, although complex, is perfectly wrought. And with several different narrative accounts, none of them entirely reliable, it's also a thoroughly modern novel, aware that it's fiction and that the reader knows it is.

COOL LITTLE TOWN...

... is how Hokitika describes itself on its website. It is well worth a visit and easily reachable from Greymouth, the main regional town, 25 miles (40km) to the north. Greymouth itself is linked with Christchurch by road and rail through the spectacular Southern Alps.

It is set during the Gold Rush in Hokitika, a town on the west coast of New Zealand's South Island. A newcomer checks in to the Crown Hotel and there encounters a dozen men who recall recent events, including the death of one man and the disappearance of another. The story is energized not only by its own complexity—sex, drugs, murder, and treachery are all writ large—but also by Catton's evident delight in telling it, not once but several times from many points of view. Moreover, the descriptions of the spectacular landscape of South Island should do much to overcome any misgivings that potential foreign visitors may have about New Zealand's remoteness and the time it takes to reach it from almost anywhere. Catton is particularly strong on the lush vegetation: she writes of places "where the mosses were fat and damp, where the leaves were waxy, where the bush was an earthy-smelling tangle, where the Nikau fronds, shed from the trunks of the palms, lay upon the ground as huge and heavy as the flukes of whales."

Some of her descriptions read like a challenge to the traveler: the coastline to the south of Okahu may be "sheer and impassable," but beyond it lie "the deep waterways of the southern fjords, where the sun set early behind the sudden peaks." It's hard to read *The Luminaries* without breaking off to check the availability of flights to Auckland.

RIGHT *Dedicated in 1903, the Hokitika Clock Tower is both a civic amenity and a memorial to the New Zealanders who gave their lives in the Boer Wars in South Africa.*

THE TENDERNESS OF WOLVES

INDEMNITY ONLY

THE AGE OF INNOCENCE

TALES OF THE CITY

CHAPTER 5

NORTH AMERICA

THE TENDERNESS OF WOLVES (2006)

STEF PENNEY

The invented setting of this novel is the isolated settlement of Caulfield on Dove River, which was inspired by various small settlements on Ontario's Georgian Bay, a large arm of Lake Huron. Or rather, to be strictly accurate, it was inspired by descriptions and photographs of them—the Scottish author, Stef Penney (b. 1969), was agoraphobic at the time and never went anywhere near Canada while writing the novel.

However, no work of the imagination should be judged by the number of stamps in its creator's passport. Penney's meticulous research has produced a picture of remote Canada in the 19th century—"a mean land that is either bog or stones, where even the willows and tamaracks cannot take hold." Her tundra has an as-it-were symbiotic relationship with the action: both become colder, harsher, and more forbidding as the story proceeds.

On the face of it, *The Tenderness of Wolves* is a murder mystery, insofar as it opens with the discovery of the body of a local fur-trapper and trader who has had his throat cut and has been scalped. But the story soon widens and deepens. Mrs Ross, who found the corpse, alerts the local magistrate, Andrew Knox, who brings in three men from the Hudson's Bay Company to help with the investigation. They are later joined by William Parker, a mixed-race trapper who is briefly a suspect but soon becomes Mrs Ross's native guide, and Thomas Sturrock, a former journalist with an interest in traditional North American native culture. Meanwhile, Mrs Ross

learns that her teenage son has disappeared. Thus when they set off along the trail of footprints leading away from the scene of the crime into the snowbound countryside, they are all seeking different objectives: the murderer, the missing boy,

the solution to an old mystery of two girls who went missing 17 years previously, and preservable relics of a rapidly disappearing way of life.

Although this book has several of the elements of a conventional whodunit, it is more an examination of the motives of those involved in the hunt. While many of the searchers may be doing the right things for the wrong reasons, those who emerge with the least credit are those who represent the interests of the big corporation.

BELOW *Georgian Bay is an arm of Lake Huron but is sometimes nicknamed "the sixth Great Lake."*

A PLACE CALLED WINTER (2015)

PATRICK GALE

In 1908, London, England, is no place for a man with gay proclivities. When Harry Cane is outed, to avoid disgrace and imprisonment he has to leave his wife and child and make a new life for himself in some distant outpost of the British Empire; he decides on Canada.

Cane's transatlantic crossing from Liverpool, England, to Halifax, Nova Scotia, is unpleasant, but nothing like as tough as what's in store for him when he starts attempting to turn virgin prairie into wheat fields. The terrain is as inhospitable as anywhere on Earth, with bitterly cold winters and relentlessly hot summers. When Harry builds a hut he has to take all weathers into account, and thus locates his privy "far enough away for hygiene but not too distant for battling to in deep snow."

The nearest major settlement, Edmonton, is 200 miles (350km) to the west. Moose Jaw, Harry's last stopover before he stakes out his plot, is more than 300 miles (500km) in the opposite direction.

A Place Called Winter by British novelist Patrick Gale (b. 1962) is a fictionalized account of the life of his great-grandfather. In the early years of the 20th century, the real Harry Cane was one of the founding settlers of this Saskatchewan town, which grew up around a station on the Grand Trunk Pacific Railway (now the Canadian National Railway). The man who built the railway line named the town after himself, perhaps through vanity but possibly because there were no local landmarks to inspire an appropriate toponym.

In a world where homosexual activity was illegal, gays were sometimes termed "inverts." But the most remarkable inversion in this novel is that the descriptions of nature, which spare few, if any, arduous details, paradoxically make Canada every bit as attractive as it appears in glossy holiday brochures. Readers may not envy those who made their homes in places where it is possible that no human had previously set foot, and they may thank their stars they weren't the ones who had to lay the ground—but the text is likely to make them want to go and see these achievements and their setting for themselves.

BELOW *Rural Saskatchewan in wintertime: a train approaches the village of Edam, which is only 60 miles (96km) from Winter—not far by Canadian standards.*

THE AGE OF INNOCENCE (1920)

EDITH WHARTON

The American writer Edith Wharton (1862–1937) won a Pulitzer Prize for *The Age of Innocence*, which depicts the high society of 1870s New York, during the "Gilded Age."

Newland Archer is all set to marry May Welland when her cousin Ellen returns from Europe to escape her brutal husband of 12 years, Count Olenski. Newland is immediately captivated by Ellen, but the qualities that he finds attractive in her are anathema to polite society: she has strong opinions and is unafraid to express them. Newland's fiancée, by contrast, is concerned only with good form—always doing the right thing, never causing a scene.

When Newland's law firm takes on Ellen as a client, he stifles his true feelings and counsels her not to divorce her husband because of the scandal it would cause. She takes his advice and leaves town. Newland and May marry. A year later, Ellen returns and a crisis is reached: Newland is on the point of telling his wife that he's leaving her when she announces that she's pregnant. Ellen moves to France.

The Archers' union is loveless but functional. By the time of May's death, "their long years together had shown [Newland] that it did not so much matter if marriage was a dull duty, as long as it kept the dignity of a duty: lapsing from that, it became a mere battle of ugly appetites."

At the end of the book, Newland's son Dallas takes his widowed father to Paris and there tries to reunite him with Ellen. Newland is having none of it, and reflects ruefully about the ease and openness with which his children's generation discuss emotional matters that in his day remained hermetically sealed. As Dallas summarizes his parents' relationship: "You never did ask each other anything, did you? And you never told each other anything. You just sat and watched each other, and guessed what was going on underneath."

Edith Wharton portrays the high society of old New York during the time of her parents and grandparents, who were themselves very much part of this class. Yet she was independent and strong-minded, a bit like Ellen in *The Age of Innocence*, and she felt suffocated by the rigid social code—so much so that she spent a lot of her life traveling in Europe, to which she moved permanently in 1913.

OCEAN STATE OUTING

Although the main setting of *The Age of Innocence* is New York City, in Chapter 21 the Archers run into Ellen by chance on an excursion to Newport, Rhode Island, which is described in detail (and where the author spent much time). This attractive city on Narragansett Bay is 180 miles (290km) from New York and can be reached without difficulty by road or by train from Penn Station (fastest journey time roughly five hours).

Wharton's portrayal of old New York is so vivid that it becomes like a character itself, and fans visiting the city often seek out locations from her novels and her life. Yet Wharton wrote in her autobiography, *A Backward Glance* (1934), that the old New York she portrayed had already vanished by the time *The Age of Innocence* was published.

A century later, even less of it can be found. Not only is the social code vastly different, but most buildings from that time have been repurposed, altered beyond recognition, or knocked down. The house where Wharton was born and brought up, at 14 West 23rd Street, still stands, but the ground floor, the site of her father's study, is currently a Starbucks. However, nearby Madison Square Park, where she played as a child under the supervision of her nursemaid, is still recognizable. Grace Church, 802 Broadway at 10th Street, where Edith Wharton had been baptized, was where Mary Welland and Newland Archer marry in *The Age of*

EDITH GOES TO HOLLYWOOD

An award-winning film adaptation of the book was released in 1993. Directed by Martin Scorsese, it starred Daniel Day-Lewis, Michelle Pfeiffer, and Winona Ryder.

Innocence. Washington Square and Gramercy Park were the boundaries of genteel society in the old New York she wrote about; and at the time that the mansions of the nouveau riche were being erected on Fifth Avenue, carriages were still proceeding up and down the avenue "at decent intervals and a decorous pace."

BELOW *The Breakers, an 1893 Vanderbilt mansion in Newport, the town where Wharton summered.*

THE GREAT GATSBY (1925)

F. SCOTT FITZGERALD

In less than a quarter of a century, this short book of only around 60,000 words went from being a near flop on first publication to an international bestseller and one of several works commonly cited as "The Great American Novel."

Set during Prohibition and the Jazz Age, it's a tale of doomed passion and adultery among a group of people who have become wealthy in a variety of ways, none shadier than the bootlegging that has enabled James Gatz, a poor boy from North Dakota, to reinvent and transform himself into Jay Gatsby, owner of one of the most luxurious mansions on Long Island.

Scott Fitzgerald (1896–1940) himself had a house on the North Shore of the island in a neighborhood named Great Neck, which in the 1920s was attracting the nouveaux riches and arrivistes and thus growing into a suburb of New York City. To the east of Great Neck on the other side of Manhasset Bay, an inlet of Long Island Sound, is Port Washington, where established families ("old money") have made their homes.

In *The Great Gatsby*, Great Neck becomes West Egg and Port Washington becomes East Egg. Gatsby lives in West Egg, from where he gazes out across Manhasset Bay with a longing for Daisy, his lost love, who is holed up unhappily married on the other side of the water.

Daisy doesn't much like West Egg, an "unprecedented 'place' that Broadway had begotten upon a Long Island fishing village." Her cousin, Nick Carraway, the narrator, who lives next door to Gatsby, has a more modulated view of the dormitory town as "a night scene by El Greco: a hundred houses, at once conventional and grotesque, crouching under a sullen, overhanging sky and a lustreless moon."

Also powerfully evoked—and of crucial significance to the tragic plot—is the highway (now State Route 25A) from Long Island to the shore of the East River. Of this celebrated approach to New York, with its wonderful sudden revelation of the Manhattan skyline, Nick remarks:

"The city seen from the Queensboro Bridge is always the city seen for the first time, in its first wild promise of all the mystery and the beauty in the world."

HOLLYWOOD'S LOVE OF GATSBY

No fewer than four films have been made of *The Great Gatsby*—in 1949, 1974 (with Robert Redford and Mia Farrow), 2000, and 2013 (with Leonardo DiCaprio and Carey Mulligan).

OHEKA CASTLE

Jay Gatsby's mansion is a composite fictional creation based partly on Long Island's Oheka Castle, which, with more than a hundred rooms, is the second-largest private home in the United States, after Biltmore in Asheville, North Carolina. Built in the 1910s for banker and philanthropist Otto Hermann Kahn (1867–1934), Oheka Castle—which is at 135 West Gate Drive, Huntington—is now a hotel open to the public, with guided tours available. It is easily reachable from downtown Manhattan by road or by Long Island Rail Road from Penn Station to Cold Spring Harbor.

BELOW *Oheka Castle isn't the only mansion F. Scott Fitzgerald had in mind, but it's the one that readers most readily associate with Gatsby.*

THEIR EYES WERE WATCHING GOD (1937)

ZORA NEALE HURSTON

Much of this novel by American author Zora Neale Hurston (1891–1960) consists of colloquial dialogue that's both African–American and of its period and place (southern Florida). Yet beyond that lies a rich and compellingly lyrical tale of a woman who's thrice unlucky in love, yet ultimately finds personal empowerment and control over her own destiny. Hurston explained that she wasn't making political statements or addressing racial injustices, since she had ceased to think in terms of race, and instead thought only in terms of individuals.

Set in the early 20th century, the story unfolds in a series of reminiscences as Janie Crawford tells her life story to her friend Pheoby Watson. In her youth, Janie was just getting the hang of sex when her grandmother happened to see her kissing a

EATONVILLE

Zora Neale Hurston spent much of her life in Eatonville, where her father was mayor, and she set many of her stories here. It was one of the first self-governing all-black towns in the country and is now the home of the Zora Neale Hurston Museum of Fine Arts at 227 East Kennedy Boulevard. The town also holds an annual arts festival named after her.

WHEN THE WIND PUT OUT THE LIGHTS

The title of the book is taken from when Janie and Tea Cake were sheltering with others in their shanties during the hurricane, and all the lights went out: "They seemed to be staring at the dark, but their eyes were watching God." The description of the ordeal is based on the author's own experience of barely surviving a hurricane in the Bahamas.

boy. The old woman was so fearful that this was the first step on the road to perdition, as it had been for her, that she lost no time in marrying Janie off to Logan Killicks, a local farmer.

Janie was young and hot-blooded and wanted affection; Logan was older and only wanted help around his farm. Lonely and unfulfilled, Janie ran away with Joe "Jody" Starks, a superficially attractive man who charmed the people of Eatonville into electing him mayor. However, he treated Janie like a cross between an employee and a chattel, getting her to run the shop but barring her from accompanying him on his official duties.

When Jody died from kidney failure, Janie inherited his property. That solved some of her problems but created others, notably a long line of suitors, most of whom she fended off until she succumbed to the charms of Vergible

"Tea Cake" Woods. Although in some ways the least suitable of all the men in her life, Tea Cake was the one Janie really wanted, and they eloped together to Jacksonville and then moved to the Everglades. Thereafter they worked in the fields, sowing and harvesting beans, until their farm was hit by the 1928 Okeechobee hurricane. In the ensuing chaos, Tea Cake was bitten by a dog and contracted rabies. The disease drove him mad and he tried to shoot Janie, but she shot him first and killed him. She was tried for murder but acquitted. Finally, she returned to Eatonville, where she tells her story to Pheoby.

THE FEDERAL WRITERS' PROJECT

This Depression-era initiative by the US government helped struggling authors by paying them to document the nation's history and culture. Among the six thousand beneficiaries of this scheme were the then-unknown Saul Bellow and John Steinbeck. Copies of Zora Neale Hurston's contribution—*Florida: A Guide to the Southernmost State* (1939)—are now rare collectors' items.

TO KILL A MOCKINGBIRD (1960)

HARPER LEE

The outline of the main plot is well known. In a small town in Alabama, Atticus Finch, a white attorney, defends Tom Robinson, a black man charged with raping a white woman. Although the accused is clearly innocent, the all-white jury convicts him; he is later shot dead while attempting to escape from prison. Among the important secondary characters is Boo Radley, a local recluse about whom there are unkind rumors and legends, none of which, as it turns out, reflects the benevolence of the real person.

Also famous is the book's publishing history. Winner of a Pulitzer Prize in 1961, it has since been translated into 40 languages and has sold more than 30 million copies. Periodic attempts to ban it have only enhanced its reputation and increased its sales. The work has been a set text in schools, not only in the United States but throughout the world. Many people pay tribute to it as a formative influence on their attitude to race relations. They often reference one of Atticus' philosophical sayings: "You never really understand a person until you consider things from his point of view… until you climb into his skin and walk around in it."

Those who dislike the book—and there are some—think that Harper Lee (1926–2016) is asking them to believe that the narrator (Atticus Finch's daughter, Jean Louise, aka Scout, who is six years old at the start of the novel and nine at

PUTTING A SMALL TOWN ON THE MAP

Founded on cotton and timber in the late 19th century and named after the fifth President of the United States, Monroeville was little known even in its own state until it appeared, lightly disguised but readily recognizable, as "Maycomb", the setting of *To Kill a Mockingbird*. Monroeville was the childhood home of both Lee and another famous writer, Truman Capote, two years her senior; they were friends and for several years near neighbors.

Monroeville today is celebrated as "the Literary Capital of Alabama." Tens of thousands of tourists come every year, all year, but particularly during May, when a dramatized version of Lee's novel is staged annually by local players. Neither Lee's nor Capote's house is still standing, but the Old Courthouse—the scene of the trial in the novel—has a museum with Lee and Capote memorabilia. Harper Lee is buried in her family plot outside Monroeville Methodist Church in Pineview Road.

the end) can write prose that resembles a synthesis of the styles of Jane Austen and Mark Twain. But Lee never tells us when Scout wrote—there is no reason to suppose she isn't looking back, recalling emotion in tranquility. In any case, knowingness is usually preferable to faux baby talk.

Other critics have objected to the characterization of the Finches' black housemaid, Calpurnia, as a contented slave (they want her to be rebellious); of the white townsfolk as benighted and invincibly ignorant rednecks (they can't all be); and of Atticus as a "white savior" (an oppressors' stereotype, said to be founded on the notion that black people cannot stand up for themselves). This last objection seems particularly odd in view of the fact that Atticus doesn't actually manage to save his client.

Art is selective: if it encompassed everything, it would be life. It is unjust to criticize Lee for not writing a different book. The one she has written is a powerful study of racism, in both its active lynch-mob and passive acquiescent forms, which captures the architecture, climate, speech patterns, and attitudes of the rural Deep South during a period of social upheaval. It is set in the 1930s but it was written in the 1950s as the Civil Rights movement was reaching a high-water mark.

The title is a reference to Atticus's stricture, "Remember it's a sin to kill a mockingbird." Another character explains this to Scout: "Mockingbirds don't do one thing but make music for us to enjoy... sing their hearts out for us. That's why it's a sin."

HARD ACT TO FOLLOW

The media attention generated by *To Kill a Mockingbird* took Harper Lee by surprise. She accompanied her publisher on the promotional trail for a while, but soon tired of the bandwagon and took herself out of the public eye for more than half a century. The 1962 triple Oscar-winning film of the book added to her fame but didn't tempt her back into public life, although she became good friends with Gregory Peck and his family after he starred in the movie. Then, in 2015, she published *Go Set a Watchman*, which was marketed as a sequel to her masterpiece but which is now generally agreed to be a first draft of *To Kill a Mockingbird*. Harper Lee died less than a year later.

TALES OF THE CITY (1978)

ARMISTEAD MAUPIN

This is the first in a series of nine novels by American writer Armistead Maupin (b. 1944). Mary Ann Singleton, a secretary from Cleveland, Ohio, visits San Francisco on vacation and likes the city so much that she decides to settle there at once.

She's about as straitlaced as it's possible to be, and this characteristic provides an effective counterpoint to all the hippy wackiness—free love, dope, right-on flower-power expressions—that she encounters in her new environment. When she moves in to a shared house in San Francisco's Russian Hill neighborhood, Mrs Madrigal, her landlady, sticks a spliff on her door as a welcome gift.

Near the center of Mary Ann's widening social circle is Mona Ramsey, who lets her gay male friend Mouse move in with her after he splits up with his boyfriend. Mouse then starts a new relationship with gynecologist Jon Fielding. Mona rekindles her old flame D'orothea Wilson, a successful model.

Another housemate is Brian Hawkins, a waiter who spends his free time trawling for willing women wherever they may be: in bars, nightclubs, and even a launderette.

For a while Mary Ann holds herself aloof from her friends' sexual antics, but she's gradually drawn into the action, first by Beauchamp, her boss's unhappily married bisexual son-in-law, and then by Norman, another of her co-tenants, known because of his general reclusiveness as "Boo Radley," a reference to the recluse in *To Kill a Mockingbird* (1960).

Tales of the City began as a column in the *San Francisco Chronicle* newspaper—Maupin had to file 800 words a day, five days a week, for a year. Recast in book form, it was so successful that the publisher demanded sequels, but that soon became difficult: the Californian hedonism that Maupin depicted so deftly in the first two volumes was destroyed by the emergence in 1981 of AIDS, originally known as "the gay plague." It is a measure of Maupin's achievement that in the seven subsequent books he addressed this mortal peril sympathetically without losing the lightness of tone that had been one of the great qualities of the original articles.

TALE TOURS

Mrs Madrigal's house is at 28 Barbary Lane, which is a lightly fictionalized version of Macondray Lane, a narrow, pedestrianized lane in the hilly heart of San Francisco. At one end is a stairway down to Taylor Street. This walking street is now a Mecca for *Tales* pilgrims, whether exploring on their own or participating in guided walking tours. The author's website provides an interactive map of sites from the series.

RIGHT *Looking out from Russian Hill—the location of Macondray Lane, on which Maupin's fictional Barbary Lane was based—toward the Coit Tower.*

INDEMNITY ONLY (1982)

SARA PARETSKY

Publishers are always looking for reasons to reject unsolicited submissions, and the typescript from Sara Paretsky (b. 1947) gave them two: some thought that her hard-boiled detective story was too much influenced by the works of Raymond Chandler, while others took the view that her setting, Chicago, had regional interest only. When the Dial Press in New York eventually took a chance on the unknown author, they reaped rich rewards: Paretsky's enduring loyalty and a series that in 2018 had reached 19 volumes.

V. I. Warshawski—the initials stand for Victoria Iphigenia, but her friends call her Vic—is a private investigator who can hardly fail to bring Chandler's gumshoe to mind. But she is more than Philip Marlowe after gender reassignment. While Chandler's hero is world-weary, sometimes wisecracking but largely taciturn, Paretsky's is consistently outspoken. Her smart-ass sarcasm ("female-chismo") often gets her into trouble—when she wonders aloud what might have provoked some hood to beat her up, an investigating policeman suggests, not unreasonably, "He probably had a bellyful of your clowning."

Chandler's weak spot was plotting. In *The Big Sleep* (1939), the chauffeur gets killed but the reader never gets told by whom (according to legend, when asked to identify the perp, the author replied, "Damned if I know"). Paretsky, by contrast, here keeps a firm hand on her narrative, ensuring that readers don't get lost in an imbroglio that involves insurance, unions, and the Mob.

In the Marlowe books, the setting, Los Angeles, is a miasma: it's there, but in the background. In *Indemnity Only*, and indeed in the subsequent volumes, Chicago is a major presence. Lesser writers mention landmarks as a cheap way of giving their stories a local habitation and a name, but Paretsky weaves them into her narrative: they're integral,

BELOW *Much of Chicago's urban rail network is elevated on stilts, which is why it's called the "L".*

WARSHAWSKI WALKS

Many of the real places in this novel and the follow-up series are in or within easy reach of the downtown area. The Pulteney Building, where V .I. has her office, is at the corner of Wabash and Monroe; the Ajax Building is at 200 South Michigan Avenue. Further afield are V. I.'s childhood home on Houston Avenue in South Chicago; the home of Peter Thayer (the murder victim) at 5462 S. Harper Avenue; and Deadstick Pond, a wetland reserve for migratory birds, which features in Paretsky's 1988 novel *Blood Shot* (US title) or *Toxic Shock* (UK title), the fifth in the Warshawski series.

never extraneous. The downtown area is also brought to life: restaurants, bars, the "L" (the elevated rapid transit system), the Loop (the business and downtown district), Division (a major street "where rich people live in beautiful old Victorian houses and apartments or enormous high-rise condominiums").

BELOVED (1987)

TONI MORRISON

Beloved is a challenging read, both thematically and stylistically. The waking nightmare of slavery is recounted in a series of flashbacks, monologues, and memories in a prose style that may justly be described as maximalist: Toni Morrison (b. 1931) has donned the mantle of William Faulkner.

The novel has several settings: a plantation in the slave state of Kentucky just after the American Civil War; a prison camp with a chain gang in Georgia; the banks of the Ohio River; and the countryside near Cincinnati, Ohio, in the abolitionist North, to which the central characters have escaped. When the action begins, they have been settled there for 18 years.

Thus Morrison shows something of the United States on both sides of the Mason–Dixon line. Yet although the fault lines in US society are among her concerns, it is uncertain that this is one of them: the South isn't all bad, just as the North isn't a paradise for black people. Similarly, the natural and the supernatural commingle here in ways that add depth and intensity to the narrative—the ghost of a child may not be a ghost at all; it is open to interpretation and has become the subject of speculation and critical studies.

This ambivalence extends to the symbolism. Take trees. The heroine, Sethe, has a scar on her back from a whipping. She is disfigured by it, and the memory of it is painful to her. But Amy Denver, a white woman who helps her during her flight, tries to turn a negative into a positive by likening the shape of it to a chokecherry tree in bloom. To Paul D., another fugitive slave, trees signpost the road to freedom. A group of Cherokee tell him to run toward blossom. Both he and Baby Suggs, Sethe's mother-in-law, confide in trees because trees won't repeat what they've heard and will never desert them. Trees represent trustworthiness and reliability in a world where both virtues are in short supply, but Sethe also recalls lynchings; "boys hanging from the most beautiful sycamores in the world."

Like almost everyone and everything in *Beloved*, Nature is ambivalent. It means different things to different people; the only certainty is its presence.

BELOVED ONSCREEN

A film of the book was released in 1998. Directed by Jonathan Demme, *Beloved* starred Oprah Winfrey, Danny Glover, and Thandie Newton.

MIDNIGHT IN THE GARDEN OF GOOD AND EVIL (1994)

JOHN BERENDT

A work of prose fiction that is all the author's invention is a novel. A work of prose that describes real events is a history book. A story that contains both elements (but more of the latter than the former) has become known as a work of faction.

In *Midnight in the Garden of Good and Evil*, American journalist John Berendt (b.1939) follows the factional lead of *In Cold Blood* (1966) by Truman Capote. Among other landmarks of this sub-genre are *Hell's Angels* (1967) by Hunter S. Thompson and several works by Norman Mailer, including *Armies of the Night* (1968), about an anti-Vietnam War march in Washington, D.C., and *The Executioner's Song* (1979), about Gary Gilmore, the American murderer who demanded—and eventually won in 1977—the right to be executed.

Berendt's book is also about a killer—Jim Williams, an antique dealer who in 1981 shot dead male prostitute Danny Hansford. After three

murder trials ended inconclusively, Williams was finally found to have acted in self-defense and was acquitted. He died in 1990.

At least as powerful as the subject matter is the setting: Savannah, Georgia, whose topography and citizens (many of them highly idiosyncratic) are here portrayed so vividly that Berendt's book became a magnet for visitors to a city that had previously been regarded by many tourists as a bit too far off the beaten track to warrant an excursion.

Two sights in particular have been popularized by *Midnight*. One is Mercer House at 429 Bull Street, the home of the shooter and the scene of the crime. It is now the Mercer-Williams House Museum.

The other sight is a statue that had no link to the case before a photograph of it was used as the cover illustration of the book. *Bird Girl*, a 1936 bronze statue by sculptor Sylvia Shaw Judson (1897–1978), had gone largely unremarked for years in Savannah's Bonaventure Cemetery but soon after publication of the book the figure became famous and its location was transformed into one of the city's most visited sites.

At first most people thought that this popularity would be a nine days' wonder, but when the image was retained on subsequent editions of the book, pedestrian traffic through the graveyard became so heavy and relentless that, in order to preserve the area's tranquility, the statue was

CIRCLE OF LIFE

Bird Girl is no longer in Bonaventure Cemetery, but the man who propelled the sculpture to global fame, photographer Jack Leigh (1948–2004), is buried there.

moved in 1997 to a more suitable location. It is now displayed in the Jepson Center for the Arts at 207 West York Street.

ABOVE *Mercer House (now a museum) was the home of Jim Williams, whose real-life killing of a male prostitute in 1981 was the basis of this book. Construction of the house began in 1860, but work was interrupted by the American Civil War (1861–65). It was completed in around 1868 and was restored by Williams a century later.*

THE GOLDFINCH (2013)

DONNA TARTT

Anyone considering a trip to Las Vegas should read this Pulitzer Prize-winning novel by American writer Donna Tartt (b. 1963), particularly from Chapter Five onward, when the hero, Theo Decker, goes to live in Las Vegas with his wastrel father. Tartt's vision of the city in the Mojave Desert is not romantic—she sees all of "its lights and rackets, its trash and daydreams, its projections and hollow facades"—but it captures the "dusty, golden quality" with a piercing and hard-to-resist clarity.

Tartt embroiders her narrative so richly that it seems to encompass almost the whole of life, even some of its coincidences and wilder improbabilities.

The novel opens with Theo, then aged 13, at the New York Metropolitan Museum of Art with his mother. She tries to infect him with her love of Dutch Renaissance painting, and particularly wants him to appreciate *The Goldfinch*, a miniature completed by Carel Fabritius shortly before he was blown up in the Delft gunpowder store explosion of 1654. Moments after she has explained that the artist was "Rembrandt's pupil, Vermeer's teacher," and that "this one little painting was really the missing link between the two of them," his mother dies in much the same way as Fabritius, when a terrorist bomb goes off in the gallery.

Theo escapes clutching the painting he has just learned about. He later considers returning it but, with almost every day that passes, the reasons for not doing so become more numerous and compelling. The longer he holds on to it, the more explaining he'll have to do if he gives it back, so

he doesn't. The rest of the story concerns Theo's struggle to straighten out his life; his problems get a lot worse before he finds their solution.

Tartt's work is routinely likened to that of Dickens, and there are some easy-to-spot similarities. Theo's mysterious guardian angel-cum-benefactor and an aloof young love object recall, respectively, Magwitch and Estella in *Great Expectations* (1860). The friendship of Theo and Boris, a street-smart Ukrainian, is reminiscent of that between Oliver Twist and the Artful Dodger. And, like almost any *Bildungsroman*, the book invites comparisons with *David Copperfield* (1850).

Yet the two authors are also very unalike in many ways, particularly in their use of detail. Dickens used a broad brush, whereas Tartt's work is much more like that of Fabritius, whose painting she describes with an aestheticism that is nowhere in the British author. Not even in Dickens's most vivid depictions of the poor did he attempt anything remotely resembling the parts of Tartt's narrative and dialogue that deal with illicit narcotic dealing and consumption.

It would be miraculous if a novel of more than 800 pages had not a word out of place, and this book is not without superfluous baggage. Occasionally, the reader might prefer a faster narrative pace to rhetorical questions such as, "How was it possible to miss someone as much as I missed my mother?" Also, the number of metaphors drawn from television and films—"a Hispanic guy who looked a lot like Luis on *Sesame Street*";

"a Bela Lugosi stare"—may be thought excessive (and exclusive, if you haven't seen the originals referred to). And when the prose goes floppy, it's hard not to recall how fundamentally far-fetched the plot is. Slack writing may be okay if the story is gripping, and good style can mitigate a shortage of action or credibility; but when both elegance and substance go missing, it's tempting to stick a bookmark between the pages and seek other forms of entertainment—such as a trip to Nevada.

BELOW *Where the action begins: the Metropolitan Museum of Art, 1000 Fifth Avenue, New York.*

BELOW *Las Vegas seen from one of the upper floors of the Cosmopolitan hotel.*

UNDER THE VOLCANO (1947)

MALCOLM LOWRY

This novel by English novelist Malcolm Lowry (1909–57) describes one day—the last day—in the life of Geoffrey Firmin, a British consul in Cuernavaca, Mexico. In *Ninety-Nine Novels: The Best in English since 1939* (1984), Anthony Burgess described Lowry's novel as "a Faustian masterpiece," and that phrase now appears on the back cover of the Penguin Modern Classics edition.

Burgess picked up on the quotations from and allusions to Christopher Marlowe's *Doctor Faustus* (1592) throughout *Under the Volcano*, starting in Chapter One with "Cut is the branch that might have grown full straight." But while the protagonist of Marlowe's play is thirsty for knowledge, Lowry's central character is just thirsty for the alcohol that will bring him what he most desires: oblivion.

As the reader gradually discovers, Geoffrey Firmin has much to want to forget. There is the unhappy childhood in India: a mother who died when he was young and a father who subsequently remarried, had another son, then abandoned

CUERNAVACA TODAY

Known as the City of Eternal Spring because of its pleasant year-round climate, Cuernavaca ("cow horn" in Spanish, a corruption of the Aztec Cuauhnahuac, meaning "place for trees,") lies 40 miles (65km) south of Mexico City, at 5,000ft (1,500m) above sea level, in the shadows of one active volcano, Popocatépetl, and another dormant one, Iztaccihuatl. A popular weekend retreat for wealthy locals from the bustle and pollution of Mexico City, Cuernavaca is easily accessible from the capital by the Pullman de Morelos bus.

all three of his dependents. There is the shady record in World War 1, with German officers in his custody mysteriously disappearing and never seen again. There is the disappointing subsequent career, as British consul in Cuernavaca, where Britons never go (he eventually resigns his post). And there is the failed marriage: his wife Yvonne left him a year previously, but returns to him on

LEFT *Mexico's active volcano Popocatépetl, visible from Cuernavaca, here looms over a church perched on top of the Great Pyramid of Cholula.*

what turns out to be the fateful day.

The ill effects of a lifetime's drinking are visible on almost every page, but they are constantly overshadowed by the Mexican scenery, which in Lowry's descriptions remains alluring, even—or perhaps especially—when the weather is at its most threatening.

A film of the same title and based on the book was released in 1984. Directed by John Huston, it starred Albert Finney as Geoffrey Firmin.

MEXICO
LIKE WATER FOR CHOCOLATE (1989)
LAURA ESQUIVEL

This international bestseller comprises 12 chapters, one per month, each of which begins with a recipe that reflects the events described and the leading character's state of mind.

Laura Esquivel (b. 1950) has here produced a courtly love-and-cuisine romance. *Like Water for Chocolate* describes the tensions between three of the main things that, depending on your view, either make the world go around or impede its motion through space: tradition, pragmatism, and passion.

Mama Elena expects Tita, her youngest daughter, to take care of her in her dotage, because that's what youngest daughters in early 20th-century Mexico are supposed to do. So she forbids the girl to marry Pedro, her one true love. She does, however, offer Pedro the hand of Rosaura, one of her older children, and Pedro accepts it in order to remain close to the one he really wants.

Over the next 22 years, the course of true love does not run smooth, but neither does it stagnate. Tita is like the sweet comestible of the title, which needs cooling while being prepared in order to prevent it from boiling and spoiling. Eleven of the recipes are for food dishes, but the month of June begins with a list of the ingredients and the method for making matches: "The gum arabic is dissolved in enough hot water to form a paste that is not too thick; when the paste is ready, the phosphorus is added and dissolved into it, and the same is done with the potassium nitrate." This is plainly a warning sign: if Tita isn't careful, she might combust.

The mother–daughter relationship deteriorates. In July, Elena decides that Tita is trying to poison her and that they therefore have to hire a cook, but the cook quits after three days. More cooks come and go. In August, Elena dies of natural causes, but even beyond the grave she continues to exert a baleful influence on Tita, appearing to her repeatedly to remind her not to go near Pedro. Yet the flesh finally proves stronger than the ghostly presence, and when the lovers finally consummate their chronic love, their passion is so fiery that it consumes them both.

Like Water for Chocolate is one of the most popular books ever published in Mexico. In translation it has increased foreign interest in authentic Mexican food and encouraged tourism.

DIRTY BLONDE AND HALF-CUBAN

WIDE SARGASSO SEA

CITY OF GOD

THE TIME OF THE HERO

CHAPTER 6

CARIBBEAN, CENTRAL, AND SOUTH AMERICA

DIRTY BLONDE AND HALF-CUBAN (2005)

LISA WIXON

Cuba is an island of contradictions. It has free universal health care, but its poor are undernourished. Its revolutionary government deplores capitalism, but its people cannot survive on the worthless local peso, so all meaningful transactions are conducted in US dollars and other hard foreign currencies.

Alysia Briggs, the American heroine of Lisa Wixon's debut novel, gathers from her mother's deathbed confession that the man she has always known as her father is not her biological parent; she was the product of an extramarital affair with a Cuban translator. Although Alysia has nothing

BELOW *A life-size bronze statue of Hemingway, by José Villa Soberón, now occupies the corner of El Floridita that the author favored in his lifetime.*

more to go on than the man's forenames—José Antonio—she sets off to socialist Neverland to reconnect with her true progenitor.

She takes with her more than enough money for her intended year's stay, but since it is well known by the locals that, because of US trade sanctions, American visitors can use only cash in Cuba, she has it all stolen almost as soon as she arrives in Havana.

To make ends meet while she searches, she becomes a high-class courtesan. In Cuba this is no disgrace because needs must; she later sees "a noble family of doctors and engineers let rooms to sex tourists for $20 a night." One of her best friends in Havana, a cardiac surgeon, does not earn enough to live on, so supplements her meager pay by providing escort services to rich foreign visitors.

WIXON ON CUBA

"Havana, a breezy city full of liveliness and music, fights the drab atmosphere the government attempts to impose… as if it were Pyongyang and not a tropical port."

★

"On an island that grows the world's greatest tobacco, imported Marlboros are inferior but expensive, and a… status symbol."

ON BEING HALF-CUBAN

Some of Wixon's sharpest observations are of the problems of being the child of a mixed marriage: Americans tend to see Alysia as Cuban, and Cubans see her as American. One of her daily difficulties is cultural references: American music and films are banned in Cuba, so when she refers to "Hotel California" (as in "You can check out any time you like/But you can never leave") or to someone being "as cheap as Jack Benny," no one knows what she's talking about.

ABOVE *Sunset on the 5-mile (8-km) esplanade known officially as Avenida de Maceo but colloquially (and almost universally) as El Malecón.*

Alysia herself has many clients, and her encounters with them make up a large part of this book.

When Alysia turns for help to Santería—the Yoruban religion that is at least partly followed by millions of Cubans—the *babalawo* (priest) tells her semi-cryptically that the rain that falls from her roof is the water her family walk in on the way to the market. This encourages her to keep looking, but it still takes her almost all the time she has available to find her father.

Readers get vivid views of Havana from both the natives' and the visitors' perspectives. Highlights include El Floridita on Calle Obispo, where they serve Hemingway daiquiris and the barmen make better money than the city's lawyers; and El Malecón, the seawall where Habaneros hang out—all human life is there. Other essential locations are the Gran Teatro García Lorca, the Parque Central, and the Casa de la Música de Miramar disco club.

WIDE SARGASSO SEA (1966)

JEAN RHYS

Although it is not essential to be familiar with *Jane Eyre* before reading *Wide Sargasso Sea*, it certainly helps, because this work by Jean Rhys (1890–1979) is a prequel to Charlotte Brontë's 1847 novel. Rhys, who was born and raised on the Lesser Antilles island of Dominica, where *Wide Sargasso Sea* is partly set, attempts to explain how Mr Rochester's first wife came to be mad and locked in the attic of his house in Yorkshire.

WHAT'S IN A NAME?

When the newlyweds visit Massacre, no one can tell them quite how the place acquired its disconcerting name. In reality this village on the west coast of Dominica memorializes an atrocity carried out there in 1674. A local chief known as Indian Warner, the son of an English knight and a native woman, wanted to protect the rights of his indigenous Carib subjects. However, his half-brother Phillip Warner, a full Englishman and Governor of Antigua, had other ideas. He sailed to Dominica and invited Indian and his people onto his ship for a reunion party. As soon as they were all on board, Phillip killed Indian; his crew did the same to all the villagers.

Rhys's heroine, Antoinette Mason, is a Creole living in Spanish Town, Jamaica, in the 1830s. (Creoles in this context are white West Indians who are discriminated against, not only by their black compatriots but also by incoming whites.) She marries an unnamed fortune-seeker (those in the know gather that this is Mr R.), who takes her back home to England. There he stops addressing her by her given name—he calls her "Bertha"—and eventually imprisons her in Thornfield Hall.

Predictably enough, Rhys's descriptions of nature are partly reflections of her characters' states of mind. In Jamaica, Antoinette knows "the time of day when though it is hot and blue and there are no clouds, the sky can have a very black look." When the couple start their honeymoon on Dominica, the bridegroom observes: "There was a soft warm wind blowing but I understood why the porter had called it a wild place. Not only wild but menacing. Those hills would close in on you."

Antoinette's reference to the black sky foreshadows her impending fate, while her husband's description of the menacing hills augurs his fear of unconstrained passion. But both passages have literal meanings, too. Rhys excels at capturing the essence of both islands: everything from sun and heat to razor grass (*Scleria scinders*) that cuts the legs and arms of passers-by.

ABOVE *Don't let the name put you off: Massacre, in Dominica, is an attractive (and safe) seaside town.*

ONE HUNDRED YEARS OF SOLITUDE (1967)

GABRIEL GARCÍA MÁRQUEZ

This is not the earliest work of magical realism but it is widely regarded as the foremost novel in the genre and at least a part of the model for many subsequent authors. The authors whom the Nobel laureate Gabriel García Márquez (1927–2014) influenced that are featured in this volume include Isabel Allende (*The House of the Spirits*, 1982, page 154), Toni Morrison (*Beloved*, 1987, page 137), Laura Esquivel (*Like Water for Chocolate*, 1989, page 143), Joanne Harris (*Chocolat*, 1999, page 42), Carlos Ruiz Zafón (*The Shadow of the Wind*, 2001, page 36), and Gina Ochsner (*The Russian Dreambook of Color and Flight*, 2009, page 69).

Magical realism may be easier to recognize than to define, but it is broadly a device that enables writers to treat obliquely subjects that were better not tackled head-on. This is sometimes an effort to avoid stereotype and cliché—as, for example, here when a son's blood flows toward his mother, an original way of conveying the notion of filial love. At other times, it may be an attempt to veil political criticism, a subterfuge that in certain circumstances under some regimes may be a survival tactic for the author. Márquez does that here in his accounts of some of the upheavals in Colombian history, notably the fictionalized version of the 1928 Banana Massacre, when the army set upon striking workers at the United Fruit Company, killing up to three thousand of them.

Much of the action in *One Hundred Years of Solitude* takes place in Macondo, a town founded by José Arcadio Buendía, whose own life and the lives of his children, grandchildren, and great-grandchildren are the main focus of the book. Although imaginary, the setting is a mirror of reality—sometimes plain, more frequently distorted to various degrees, but always with a kernel of poetic truth. When Macondo gets its first cinema, local audiences struggle to work out how an actor who died at the end of one week's main feature can live again in the following presentation.

Eventually Macondo's isolation is ended by the construction of a railway line, along which comes an unstoppable flow of gringos and gringo influences. And then there's a hurricane that wipes the town off the face of the Earth.

THE REAL MACONDO

Macondo is modelled on Márquez's birthplace, Aracataca, near Colombia's Caribbean coast. It is a little over 400 miles (650km) north of Bogotá as the crow flies, or about 540 miles (875km) by car. The nearest city is Santa Marta 50 miles (80km) away. The town of Macondo boasts a modest museum of the author's life and work and a statue of Remedios the Beauty, in the book a great-granddaughter of the founder of Macondo, José Arcadio Buendía.

CITY OF GOD (1997)

PAULO LINS

Cidade de Deus, meaning "City of God", is the name given to a 1960s' social housing project that aimed to get the poor out of the slums (favelas) of central Rio de Janeiro into better accommodation on the outskirts of the city.

In 1966, heavy rain brought severe flooding to the older poor areas. Many of their occupants fled to Cidade de Deus, which soon housed 40,000 people, many more than originally intended. Under-financed, it soon became another—and by general agreement the most violent and corrupt—of Rio's 600 favelas.

TOURISM AND POVERTY TOURISM

The statue of Christ the Redeemer on Corcovado peak, Sugarloaf Mountain, Copacabana and Ipanema beaches, the Jardim Botânico, the Lapa neighborhood, Tijuca National Park, the Maracanã Stadium… there are many famous sights in Rio that the Brazilian Tourist Board is anxious for everyone to see. One of the original aims of Cidade de Deus was to get the poor out of sight: they were thought to be bad for business. Today, however, guided tours of the favelas are widely available and popular with visitors from all over the world. Note that it is a bad idea to enter these districts either alone or (by most accounts especially) at the invitation of a new acquaintance who lives there.

Paulo Lins (b. 1958) grew up in Cidade de Deus, the son of a house painter and a domestic helper. He based this book on his childhood observations of a ghetto in which prostitution, theft, torture, rape, and murder are everyday occurrences. Most of his cast of more than 300 characters are practitioners and/or victims of at least one of these crimes. Although his work is principally a description of mayhem, it also offers insights into the hierarchies and honor systems of some of the most deprived sections of Brazilian society.

City of God was an instant success in Portuguese, but because so much of the dialogue is in the argot of the shantytown, it was thought at first to be untranslatable. But then the 2002 film version, co-directed by Fernando Meirelles and Kátia Lund, became a worldwide hit and made foreign-language editions of the book commercially imperative. The 2006 English translation by Australian Alison Entrekin succeeds well in rendering Brazilian favelaspeak into street-credible English.

BELOW *From rags to riches in a single image: the impoverished City of God in the foreground is backed by the high-rise office blocks of wealthy downtown Rio.*

THE TIME OF THE HERO (1963)

MARIO VARGAS LLOSA

This debut novel from Mario Vargas Llosa (b. 1936) depicts brutality at the Leoncio Prado Military Academy in Lima, an establishment the author himself attended in the 1940s. At the time of publication, the Peruvian government denounced the novel as enemy propaganda, and the academy bought a thousand copies of the first edition and ritualistically burned them.

Since the Leoncio Prado was Peru's top military academy, it is not completely surprising that the country's rulers should have taken against the book. If violence engenders violence, there's plenty of it on these pages to provoke extreme responses.

The Spanish title is *La ciudad y los perros* ("The City and the Dogs"). The "dogs" are the new recruits, who are subjected to cruelty in order to toughen them up; those who survive the first year get to be cruel to the following year's intake. One third-year cadet steals some examination papers. Another grasses him up to the officers and soon afterward gets shot dead during a training exercise, perhaps by accident but possibly as an act of vengeance.

The shooter, known as Jaguar, is a nasty piece of work who had a criminal record before he enrolled at the school. He denies involvement and is cleared by an internal investigation. Two young soldiers—one a cadet, the other a supportive lieutenant—try to nail him, but the establishment closes ranks and thwarts their efforts.

The turning point comes when Jaguar gets waylaid by a gang of recruits who mistakenly believe that he's an informer. Now aware as never before of the pain of injustice, Jaguar starts to see himself as others see him. It would be wrong to spoil the surprising ending; suffice it to say that the book's epigraph is a quotation from the philosopher Jean-Paul Sartre. At the core of *The Time of the Hero* is the existentialist notion that a criminal yesterday is not a criminal today, because guilt is in the past and we live only in the present.

OPPOSITE *The suggested walking route passes through this park, named* La Pera del Amor *(The Pear of Love), with its distinctive mosaic seating.*

VARGAS LLOSA'S LIMA

The Colegio Militar Leoncio Prado—motto: Discipline, Morality and Work—looks out over the Pacific at Avenida Costanera 1541, La Perla. From there, keep the ocean on your right until the Parque La Pera del Amor, then head inland through the Miraflores district, where the author spent childhood weekends with his father. (He lived during the week with his mother in Peru's second city, Arequipa.) Next, proceed east along the Avenida Angamos Oeste, which becomes the Avenida Angamos Este and then Avenida Primavera, where "between that double row of mansions, each with its broad, carefully tended garden… tangles of light and shadow… ran up and down the trunks of the trees or quivered in the boughs."

CHILE

THE HOUSE OF THE SPIRITS (1982)

ISABEL ALLENDE

The setting of *The House of the Spirits* is never named, but there is no doubt that it is Chile. Of the main characters, "the Candidate" (later "the President") is Salvador Allende, Chile's head of state for three years from 1970 (and the author's second cousin and godfather). "General Hurtado" is a fictionalized Augusto Pinochet, the military dictator who overthrew Allende in 1973 and ruled until 1990. "The Poet" is Pablo Neruda, Chilean winner of the 1971 Nobel Prize in Literature, who died less than two weeks after the coup d'état.

Isabel Allende (b. 1942) is proud of her country, which she has described as "a wild paradise of cold forest, volcanoes, lakes and rivers." She maintains that this novel is "a portrait of Latin America, not only Chile": she wants to keep readers mindful of the possibility that the events she describes could happen anywhere on the continent.

Or at least the political events could—*The House of the Spirits* is one of the great landmarks of magical realism, the literary genre characterized by the periodic infiltration of supernatural occurrences into broadly realistic contexts. Within the first few pages, we meet a man who builds a mechanical bird on which he flies off into the mountains, a dog that grows to the size of a horse, and a child who can both foretell the future and perform telekinesis.

Such characters and incidents interlard this three-generational saga of the Trueba family. Clara the Clairvoyant marries Esteban Trueba, landowner, conservative senator, and serial rapist. Their daughter, Blanca, has a sexless marriage with a porn-loving Frenchman; Blanca's daughter, Alba, is fathered by Pedro Tercero García, a left-wing activist (another character based on a real person: Víctor Jara, poet and songwriter, killed in the early days of the Pinochet regime).

In addition to enlivening a story that might otherwise be drily historico-political, magical realism serves as a means of expressing the inexpressible. It is effective in many contexts, especially in works like *The House of the Spirits* set in or written under totalitarian regimes that are wont to punish open criticism with torture and death.

CEMETERY MONUMENTS

The Cementerio General de Santiago is one of the world's largest graveyards, with more than two million bodies interred there. Among the many striking works of funerary art on the 210-acre (85-hectare) plot are memorials to President Allende and Los Desaparecidos—the people who vanished without trace under the military junta. The cemetery is easily reachable from the center of Santiago on Linea 2 of the city Metro.

FURTHER READING

Here are some suggestions for other novels which may inspire you to visit their locations, or provide useful background knowledge before you travel.

Afghanistan
James A. Michener (1907–97): *Caravans* (1963)
Elliot Ackerman (b. 1980): *Green on Blue* (2015)

Albania
William Peter Blatty (1928–2017): *Dimiter* (2010)

Armenia
Khachatur Abovian (1809–48): *Wounds of Armenia* (1841/1858)

Australia
Patrick White (1912–90): *The Tree of Man* (1955)
Thomas Keneally (b. 1935): *The Chant of Jimmie Blacksmith* (1972)

Austria
Arthur Schnitzler (1862–1931): *Dream Story* (1926)
Joseph Roth (1894–1939): *The Radetzky March* (1932)

Botswana
Bessie Head (1937–86): *When Rain Clouds Gather* (1968)
Will Randall (b. 1966): *Botswana Time* (2006)

Brazil
Raduan Nassar (b. 1935): *Ancient Tillage* (1975)

Canada
L.M. Montgomery (1874–1942): *Anne of Green Gables* (1908)
Leonard Cohen (1934-2016): *The Favourite Game* (1963)
Michael Ondaatje (b. 1943): *In the Skin of a Lion* (1987)

Chile
Roberto Bolaño (1953–2003): *Distant Star* (1996)
Alejandro Zambra (b. 1975): *Ways of Going Home* (2011)

China
Cao Xueqin (c. 1715–c. 1764): *Dream of the Red Chamber* (1791)
Mo Yan (b. 1955): *Red Sorghum* (1986)

Colombia
José Eustasio Rivera (1888–1928): *The Vortex* (1924)
Fernando Vallejo (b. 1942): *Our Lady of the Assassins* (1994)

Croatia
Ivo Andrić (1892–1975): *The Bridge on the Drina* (1945)
Aminatta Forna (b. 1964): *The Hired Man* (2013)

Cuba
Oscar Hijuelos (1951–2013): *The Mambo Kings Play Songs of Love* (1989)

Denmark
Lois Lowry (b. 1937): *Number the Stars* (1989)
Rose Tremain (b. 1943): *Music and Silence* (1999)

Egypt
Agatha Christie (1890–1976): *Death on the Nile* (1937)
Waguih Ghali (c. 1924–69): *Beer in the Snooker Club* (1964)

England
Thomas Hardy (1840–1928): *The Return of the Native* (1878)
Graham Greene (1904–91): *Brighton Rock* (1938)

France
Charles Dickens (1812–70): *A Tale of Two Cities* (1859)
Irène Némirovsky (1903–1942): *Suite Française* (2004)

Germany
Erich Maria Remarque (1898–1970): *All Quiet on the Western Front* (1929)
Markus Zusak (b. 1975): *The Book Thief* (2005)

Greece
Nikos Kazantzakis (1883–1957): *Zorba the Greek* (1946)
John Fowles (1926–2005): *The Magus* (1965)

Greenland
Jane Smiley (b. 1949): *The Greenlanders* (1988)

India
Salman Rushdie (b. 1947): *Midnight's Children* (1981)
Vikram Seth (b. 1952): *A Suitable Boy* (1993)

Iran
Sadegh Hedayat (1903–51): *The Blind Owl* (1936)
Iraj Pezeshkzad (b. 1928): *My Uncle Napoleon* (1973)

Ireland
Edna O'Brien (b. 1930): *The Country Girls* (1960)
William Trevor (1928–2016): *The Story of Lucy Gault* (2002)

Israel
Batya Gur (1947–2005): *Murder on a Kibbutz* (1991)
Meir Shalev (b. 1948): *A Pigeon and a Boy* (2006)

Italy
Umberto Eco (1932–2016): *The Name of the Rose* (1980)
Donna Leon (b. 1942): *Death at La Fenice* (1992)

Jamaica
Richard Hughes (1900–76): *A High Wind in Jamaica* (1929)
Marlon James (b. 1970): *A Brief History of Seven Killings* (2014)

Japan
Jun'ichiro Tanizaki (1886–1965): *The Makioka Sisters* (1948)
James Clavell (1921–94): *Shōgun* (1975)

Kenya
M. M. Kaye (1908–2004): *Death in Kenya* (1958)
Meja Mwangi (b. 1948): *Kill Me Quick* (1973)

Mexico
B. Traven (c. 1882–1969): *The Treasure of the Sierra Madre* (1927)
Carlos Fuentes (1928–2012): *The Death of Artemio Cruz* (1962)

Mongolia
Frank Cottrell-Boyce (b. 1959): *The Unforgotten Coat* (2011)

Netherlands
Harry Mulisch (1927–2010): *The Assault* (1982)
Tracy Chevalier (b. 1962): *Girl with a Pearl Earring* (1999)

New Zealand
Keri Hulme (b. 1947): *The Bone People* (1984)

Nigeria
Ben Okri (b. 1959): *The Famished Road* (1991)

Northern Ireland
Deirdre Madden (b. 1960): *One by One in the Darkness* (1996)
Anna Burns (b. 1962): *Milkman* (2018)

Norway
Tarjei Vesaas (1897–1970): *The Ice Palace* (1963)
Jo Nesbø (b. 1960): *The Snowman* (2007)

Peru
Thornton Wilder (1897–1975): *The Bridge of San Luis Rey* (1927)

Portugal
Pascal Mercier (b. 1944): *Night Train to Lisbon* (2004)
Yann Martel (b. 1963): *The High Mountains of Portugal* (2016)

Russia
Mikhail Bulgakov (1891–1940): *The Master and Margarita* (1940)
Boris Pasternak (1890–1960): *Dr Zhivago* (1957)

Saudi Arabia
Hilary Mantel (b. 1952): *Eight Months on Ghazzah Street* (1988)
Zoe Ferraris (b. 1972): *The Night of the Mi'raj* (2008)

Scotland
Alasdair Gray (b. 1934): *Lanark* (1981)
Ali Smith (b. 1962): *Girl Meets Boy* (2007)

South Africa
Alan Paton (1903–88): *Cry, the Beloved Country* (1948)
Barbara Trapido (b. 1941): *Frankie and Stankie* (2003)

Spain
Miguel de Cervantes (1547–1616): *Don Quixote* (1605)
Pedro Antonio de Alarcón (1833–1891): *The Three-Cornered Hat* (1874)

Sweden
August Strindberg (1849–1912): *The Red Room* (1879)
Stieg Larsson (1954–2004): *The Girl with the Dragon Tattoo* (2008)

Switzerland
Philip Pullman (b. 1946): *Count Karlstein* (1982)

Thailand
Stephen Leather (b. 1956): *Private Dancer* (2005)

Turkey
Elif Shafak (b. 1971): *The Bastard of Istanbul* (2006)
Yoşar Kemal (1923–2015): *Memed, My Hawk* (1955)

United States of America
Mark Twain (1835–1910): *Adventures of Huckleberry Finn* (1885)
Margaret Mitchell (1900–1949): *Gone with the Wind* (1936)

Vietnam
James Webb (b. 1946): *Fields of Fire* (1978)

Wales
Malcolm Pryce (b. 1960): *Aberystwyth Mon Amour* (2001)

Zimbabwe
Tsitsi Dangarembga (b. 1959): *Nervous Conditions* (1988)

INDEX

PICTURE CREDITS